The Challenges of No Child Left Behind

Understanding the Issues of Excellence, Accountability, and Choice

E. Jane Irons and Sandra Harris

Rowman & Littlefield Education
Lanham • New York • Toronto • Plymouth, UK
2007

Published in the United States of America
by Rowman & Littlefield Education
A Division of Rowman & Littlefield Publishers, Inc.
A wholly owned subsidary of The Rowman & Littlefield Publishing Group, Inc.
4501 Forbes Boulevard, Suite 200, Lanham, Maryland 20706
www.rowmaneducation.com

Estover Road
Plymouth PL6 7PY
United Kingdom

British Library Cataloguing in Publication Information Available

Library of Congress Cataloging-in-Publication Data

Irons, E. Jane.
  The challenges of No Child Left Behind : understanding the issues of
excellence, accountability, and choice / E. Jane Irons and Sandra Harris.
      p. cm.
  Includes bibliographical references and index.
  ISBN-13: 978-1-57886-517-8 (cloth : alk. paper)
  ISBN-10: 1-57886-517-4 (cloth : alk. paper)
  ISBN-13: 978-1-57886-518-5 (pbk. : alk. paper)
  ISBN-10: 1-57886-518-2 (pbk. : alk. paper)
  1. Educational accountability—United States. 2. Educational change—United
States. 3. Education—Standards—United States. 4. United States. No Child
Left Behind Act of 2001. I. Harris, Sandra, 1946– II. Title.
  LB2806.22.I76 2007
  379.1'580973—dc22   2006016511

⊗™ The paper used in this publication meets the minimum requirements of
American National Standard for Information Sciences—Permanence of Paper
for Printed Library Materials, ANSI/NISO Z39.48-1992.
Manufactured in the United States of America.

Contents

Preface

While our interest in school reform in general and the NCLB legislation in particular is professional, it is also personal. Since each of our first teaching experiences were very similar, we begin this book with a brief telling of one of them. Here is Jane's story:

My public school teaching career began in 1971 when I moved to Texas from Florida. My first assignment was to teach 9th grade basic mathematics in a large urban high school with grades 10 through 12. At that time, I did not understand the significance of teaching basic math. The students had accumulated little, if any, high school credit so they were assigned to 9th grade math. My teaching preparation was university-based, with an internship in a local high school teaching introduction to calculus, analytic geometry, and advanced algebra to 11th- and 12th-graders. I had no experience and little preparation to teach basic math skills.

The high school where I taught was a large urban school with over 2,800 students. The student body was about 40 percent African American and 47 percent Hispanic. The majority of my students were males with high absentee and tardy rates. Most seemed to lack motivation and were often encouraged by faculty and administration to drop out when they reached age 16. I remember visiting parents in federally assisted housing units to obtain signatures on forms for school impact aid.

In those days the school district provided modified text books that contained little reading and no problem solving. The material looked like basic skills work sheets at about a 4th grade level. The reward for completing seat work was more of the same. Direct instruction methodology was the practice and little was expected of the students. I taught at that high school for more than three years and that teaching experience refocused my educational interests to include best practices for disadvantaged students and students with disabilities.

We know that most of us as educators have had similar discouraging experiences—wanting to help students but finding it far more difficult than we ever imagined. Along with our personal commitment to serving young people and our willingness to do what it takes, school reform in its many different aspects represents our professional commitment. The winds of reform are ever-changing, and whether gentle or turbulent, they are always blowing and rarely do they provide smooth sailing. Today's reform, The No Child Left Behind Act, is gusting through our schools. It is our job as educators to navigate these churning waters to provide a safe harbor of achievement for our nation's children.

Introduction

A ship in port is safe, but that's not what ships are built for.

—Navy Admiral Grace Hopper

Educators need to get used to the idea of change and reform. After all, we live in a changing world and education is a reflection of that world. National education leaders, presidents, and the general public who advocate for public educational reform understand this and recognize that reform movements are important catalysts to progress. While equity has often been a central focus of reform, over the past twenty years it has emerged as a driving force for high-quality education for all of America's children. Quotations from three former Secretaries of Education and President George W. Bush highlight the framework for education legislation designed as the most recent catalyst for reform.

> Schools of the future will involve parents, will empower principals and teachers, will emphasize early childhood education, and will strengthen curriculum in mathematics, science, English, foreign languages, and social sciences. Most of all, schools of the future will have more sensitivity to the differing needs of an increasingly diverse population. (Cavazos 2002, p. 690)
>
> —Lauro F. Cavazos, secretary of education 1988–1990

As we look to the future, it is imperative that we recognize that our national effort to raise standards is not just about testing. Rather, it represents a broad and sweeping endeavor to reform American education from top to bottom. An unflinching commitment to excellence and equity must be our guiding principle. (Riley 2002, p. 700)

—Richard W. Riley, secretary of education 1993–2001

With the No Child Left Behind law, education reform has grown up. No longer is reform about access or money. No longer is it about compliance or excuses. Instead, it is about improving student achievement by improving the quality of the education we offer our students. It is once again focused on the student, not the system. (Paige 2002, p. 710)

—Rod Paige, secretary of education 2001–2004

Under the No Child Left Behind Act, standards are higher, test scores are on the rise, and we're closing the achievement gap for minority students (Bush 2005).

—George W. Bush, President, March 2005

These quotations from former secretaries of education and President George W. Bush clearly express the national motivation that formulated the basis of twenty-first-century reform—the legislation reauthorizing the Elementary and Secondary Education (ESEA) Act called No Child Left Behind (NCLB). With the passage of the NCLB Act of 2001, the legislature has mandated systemwide change for America's public schools (U.S. Department of Education 2002).

Because today's educators are charged with the responsibility and accountability for implementing the NCLB Act in their schools, they must create a learning community that emphasizes success for all students. Parent input must be solicited. Knowledge of the political background and the specific components of the NCLB Act are crucial for successful leadership, decision making, communication, and implementation. Additionally, educators need sources of information concerning research and best practices at their fingertips.

In an effort to support educators in navigating the waters of the NCLB reform effort, this book reviews current literature and discusses major concepts associated with this legislation. We begin with a discussion of the historical background, including major concepts of accountability and achievement. The chapters are organized in the following manner:

- Changing Accountability Measures and Achievement
- Adequate Yearly Progress (AYP)
- Highly Qualified Teachers
- Title I: Overview
- Title I: Reading and Early Childhood
- NCLB and School Reform: Charters and Vouchers
- Restructuring
- Impact of NCLB on School Finance
- High School Reform and Other Future Trends.

Additionally, each chapter includes a set of reflective questions to help readers consider their experience with NCLB and also how best to use chapter content in their own school or district. Each chapter concludes with Internet websites as a resource for accessing additional information.

1

Changing Accountability Measures and Achievement

Embarking on a cruise, or even a day sail, is an exciting and complex event.

—Roland Barth, educator and author

Traditionally, school accountability was viewed from a bean-counting mentality. Spending was reviewed with respect to state/federal mandates. Payroll expenditures were examined to ensure that individuals' salaries matched the federal program of employment. Materials, supplies, expenditures for building use, and other costs were also matched to programs. Compliance accountability reports did not address student performance or learning. In 1983, the National Commission on Excellence published the Nation at Risk Report which addressed the lack of student progress in achievement areas, particularly in math and science. This report raised public awareness of perceived failures of public education and set the stage for public demand for educational change and reform (Yudof et al. 2002).

NATIONAL GOALS

In his 1990 State of the Union address, then President George H. W. Bush made public six national performance goals for education, which included the following accountability framework:

- Preschool readiness must be addressed as students must enter school ready to learn;
- High schools must have a 90 percent graduation rate;
- Curriculum must focus on core content and include problem-solving skills;
- Schools must increase student status to become first in the world in the areas of mathematics and science;
- Schools must ensure that all students become literate citizens in a global economy;
- Public schools must be safe and drug-free.

Goals 2000

The national goals announced by George H. W. Bush formed the political platform for the 2000 Education Act passed under President Bill Clinton (Cavazos 2002). Goals 2000 embraced educational reform and change efforts by requiring the states to develop state curriculum standards and instructional practices and conduct a periodic student achievement assessment related to the national goals. Instead of only examining school inputs such as salaries, accountability now focused upon student achievement outcomes. Focusing on accountability shifted responsibility for compliance to schools and individual principals and teachers rather than either state or district levels. The Goals 2000 Act also provided funding to states to develop improvement plans to meet the national education goals (Yudof et al. 2002).

State Accountability Systems

During the 1990s fifty different complex state accountability systems emerged. Based on local interpretations of the national goals for education, each state designed a system of multiple interacting components to include tests, grade levels and subjects tested, benchmark levels of performance, public reporting and parent input, rewards and sanctions for not meeting state proficiency levels, and specific assistance for low-performing schools (Scheurich, Skrla, and Johnson 2000; Quality Counts '99, 1999; Quality Counts 2001).

Because of the many diverse state accountability systems, we have selected seven different systems to show the variances among state accountability system components based on information provided in *Education Week* for their fifth annual fifty-state report in 2001: California, Connecticut, Kentucky, New York, Texas, Utah, and Virginia. Throughout the book we refer to "selected" states. These seven states have been purposefully selected in order to demonstrate the wide impact of NCLB on implementation and achievement outcomes.

- California identified 3,144 low-performing schools. Other components were targeted for implementation in 2004.
- Connecticut identified 28 low-performing schools and utilized student test scores to compare schools by set standards and their past performance.
- Kentucky assigned ratings to all schools and identified 149 low-performing schools based on student test scores. Kentucky also collected data on attendance, dropout, and graduation rates. State-set standards and past school performance were used for school accountability comparisons.
- New York identified 105 low-performing schools, collected dropout and graduation rate data, and compared school scores with each other as well as using state standards.
- Texas assigned ratings to all schools and identified 146 low-performing schools. Texas collected dropout and graduation rate data and utilized state standards for comparisons.
- Utah did not have a well developed accountability system, although they specified by the year 2004 they would identify low-performing schools and collect test data.
- Virginia assigned an accountability rating to all schools and identified 736 low-performing schools. Virginia used state-set standards and past school performance to compare schools.

Table 1.1 shows the differences among accountability systems being developed by the different states.

State Assessment Development—Selected States

Table 1.2 shows state differences in types of tests. In general, the seven selected states used multiple choice tests to assess across all levels of elementary, middle, and high schools. For example, California and Virginia did not use short answer tests while Texas only used short answer tests at the high school level. California used extended response tests in English at the elementary and middle school level, while Utah used this type of test at the middle and high school levels. Only Kentucky used portfolio assessment across all levels.

Test content also varied across the states. For example, English content for mathematics was tested across all levels by all selected states. However, history and social science tests were not used in Utah at all, while their use varied in other states. Only Kentucky, New York, Utah, and Virginia tested science across all levels. Only Kentucky and New York involved classroom teachers in grading state accountability tests.

Targeted Assistance and Reward Development

Targeting assistance and acknowledging successful schools with rewards differed by state. For example:

- All selected states except Utah required an on-site external team to provide assistance to schools.
- Connecticut, New York, Texas, and Virginia provided assistance to all low-performing schools.
- California and Kentucky provided assistance to some low-performing schools.
- Connecticut and New York provided extra funds to all low-performing schools.
- California and Kentucky provided some funds to low-performing schools.
- Only New York required professional development for low-performing schools.

Table 1.1. State Accountability System Components—Selected States

State	Assigns Ratings to All Schools	Identifies Low-performing Schools Only	Number of Schools Judged Low-performing in 1999	Student Test Scores	Attendance Rates	Dropout/ Graduation Rates	Compares School Scores with Each Other	Compares Schools to Set Standards or Cut-off	Compares Schools with Past Performance
California		✓	3,144	2004	2004	2004			
Connecticut		✓	28	✓				✓	✓
Kentucky	✓		149	✓	✓	✓		✓	✓
New York		✓	105	✓		✓	✓	✓	
Texas	✓		146	✓		✓			
Utah		2004		2004					
Virginia	✓		736	✓				✓	✓

Source: Quality Counts (2001, pp. 80–81)

Table 1.2. State Assessment Development—Selected States

State	Multiple Choice	Short Answer	Extended Response English	Portfolio	English	Math	History/ Social Studies	Science	Classroom Teachers Involved in Grading Tests	Feedback Provided Teachers Item Analysis	Student Answers
California	ES, MS, HS		ES, MS		ES, MS, HS	ES, MS, HS	HS	HS			✓
Connecticut	ES, MS, HS	ES, MS, HS	ES, MS, HS		ES, MS, HS	ES, MS, HS	HS	HS			
Kentucky	ES, MS, HS	ES, MS, HS	ES, MS, HS	ES, MS, HS	ES, MS, HS	ES, MS, HS	ES, MS, HS	ES, MS, HS	✓	✓	
New York	ES, MS, HS	ES, MS, HS	ES, MS, HS		ES, MS, HS	ES, MS, HS	ES, MS, HS	ES, MS	✓	✓	✓
Texas	ES, MS, HS	HS	ES, MS, HS		ES, MS, HS	ES, MS, HS	MS, HS	ES, MS, HS			
Utah	ES, MS, HS	MS, HS	MS, HS		ES, MS, HS	ES, MS, HS		ES, MS, HS			
Virginia	ES, MS, HS		ES, MS, HS		ES, MS, HS	ES, MS, HS	ES, MS, HS	ES, MS, HS			✓

Source: Quality Counts (2001, pp. 74–75)

- New York and Virginia required low-performing schools to adopt a research-based program.
- Only Texas rewarded successful schools with money based on state-set targets.
- California, Connecticut, Kentucky, Texas, and Utah rewarded schools with money based on improvement.
- California, Texas, and Utah also allowed part of the state reward money to be used for teacher bonuses.

Rewards and Sanctions. Under the NCLB Act, accountability systems assume that measuring achievement and linking it to rewards and sanctions motivate schools and individuals who work in them to increase student achievement. Traditionally, the major threat for noncompliance was for states to withhold federal funds. However, withholding funds rarely occurred because students would suffer. Under NCLB sanctions, such as requiring schools to facilitate school choice by notifying the community of the school's low performance status, notifying parents of their option to select a higher-performing school in the district and providing transportation to the school of choice are becoming more common. Additional sanctions have included school reorganizations and school closures (Elmore and Fahrman 2001; Quality Counts '99, 1999; Quality Counts 2001; U.S. Department of Education 2002).

Rewards and Sanctions Development—Selected States. New York and Texas recognized that the state had the authority to close, reconstitute, or take over failing schools or to replace individual principals or teachers in failing schools. Kentucky and Texas permitted students to transfer to higher-performing schools. New York and Virginia revoked accreditation. In fact by 2001, New York had closed twelve schools and re-staffed another fifty, while Texas had taken over three schools.

States also vary on their focus for low performance. For example, Texas uses an absolute standard that is raised year by year. Virginia has set an accreditation standard that is ambitious but allows schools several years to achieve it.

Student Achievement

High level skills and knowledge are considered important for success in today's economy and society in general. Yet, schools have traditionally focused on students who are high achieving, thus creating gaps among various subgroups to include students from poverty, students with disabilities, and students whose native language is not English (Wiener and Hall 2004). The passage of the NCLB Act provided states with funding resources and some flexibility to promote accountability and challenged states to improve their education systems by holding their schools accountable for raising student achievement (National Governors Association Center for Best Practices 2005).

In addition to the annual state-developed assessments in reading, mathematics, and science, states are required to participate in biennial National Assessment of Educational Progress (NAEP) assessments in reading and mathematics for 4th- and 8th-graders beginning in 2002–2003. Policymakers are able to utilize national level NAEP data to compare the rigor of state assessments (U.S. Department of Education 2002).

Based on information provided by the Digest of Educational Statistics (2004), the NAEP has conducted assessments at the state level, since 1990. State assessment content was identical to national assessment content, but separate representative state samples were selected for each state prior to 2002. A combined sample of public schools was selected for both state and national NAEP assessments.

NAEP Reading: State Results. Fourth grade NAEP reading scale scores show the following trends using the years 1994, 1998, and 2002. State scores are compared across that same state's reported scores.

- National NAEP reading scores decreased 1 point.
- California's scores increased 9 points.
- Connecticut's scores increased 6 points.
- Kentucky's scores increased 7 points.
- New York's scores increased 10 points.
- Texas's scores increased 3 points.
- Utah's scores increased 2 points.
- Virginia's scores increased 10 points.

In general, achievement gains appear modest. Average scale scores for white, non-Hispanic students showed a higher range than when minority populations were included. The scores ranged from a difference of six points across Utah's scores to a difference of 27 points across California's scores. The 2003 main NAEP reading assessments found 4th grade reading proficiency varied widely among states with an average scale score of 216, which is nine points higher than the average scale score of 207 reported in 2002 (Digest of Education Statistics 2004).

2005 Reading and Math NAEP State Achievement Levels. The NAEP state achievement levels for reading and mathematics were published in October 2005. Table 1.3 depicts the percentages reported by selected states for each proficiency level for grade 4 reading along with the average scale score reported by the states. It should be noted that the term *proficiency* differs according to each state's definition. Differences could include test content, type of test items, test rigor, and differences in how cutoff scores were determined.

Table 1.4 shows the percentage of students reported by selected states for each proficiency level for grade 4 mathematics. The average scale score is also reported (National Center for Education Statistics 2005).

NCLB ACHIEVEMENT GAINS

Then Secretary of Education, Margaret Spellings, stated that new data on the nation's report card confirmed that NCLB was on the right track. However, the October 19, 2005, release showed mixed results. Fourth

Table 1.3. NAEP Reading: State Results—Grade 4 Achievement Levels (Percentages) (2005)

State	Average Score	Below Basic	Basic	Proficient	Advanced
National (Public)	217	38	33	23	7
California	207	50	29	17	5
Connecticut	226	29	32	27	12
Kentucky	220	35	34	23	7
New York	223	31	36	26	8
Texas	219	30	35	29	6
Utah	225	32	34	27	8
Virginia	226	28	35	29	8

Note: Detail may not sum to totals because of rounding.

Source: Based on information published by National Center for Education Statistics (2005, Oct.)

Table 1.4.   NAEP Mathematics: State Results—Grade 4 Achievement Levels (Percentages) (2005)

State	Average Score	Below Basic	Basic	Proficient	Advanced
National (Public)	237	21	44	30	5
California	230	29	43	24	4
Connecticut	242	16	42	36	7
Kentucky	231	25	49	24	3
New York	238	19	45	32	4
Texas	242	13	47	36	5
Utah	239	17	46	33	4
Virginia	240	17	43	34	6

Note: Detail may not sum to totals because of rounding.

Source: National Center for Education Statistics (2005)

grade reading rose only one point over the past two years and dropped one point for 8th grade. Olson (2005, October 26) reported that reading scores for both 4th- and 8th-graders have remained relatively the same since 1994. Sixty-four percent of 4th-graders and 73 percent of 8th-graders were reported at or above basic and 31 percent in both grades scored at or above proficient.

In math, 4th grade gained 3 points and 8th grade gained one point. Eighty percent of the fourth grade and 69 percent of the 8th grade scored at the basic level, while 36 percent of 4th grade and 30 percent of 8th grade scored at the proficient level in mathematics.

African American 4th-graders gained two points in reading and four points in math between 2003 and 2005. Hispanic 4th-graders gained three points in reading and four points in math. Although achievement between minority students has increased a few points, minority groups are still more than 20 points behind (Olson 2005, October 26, p. 22).

English Language Learners' Achievement

Based on results of the Department of Education's (DOE) first evaluation of how states are meeting requirements for English language learners (ELL), all fifty states have developed standards for English proficiency and aligned them with academic content standards. Before NCLB implementation only seven states had standards that were not linked to academic content (Zehr 2005).

The report generated by the DOE found that twenty-two states met the annual achievement objectives in learning English and attaining fluency in English. Upon examination of reading and math content, ELL student proficiency in math was met by only five states for 2003–2004 and only two states, Alabama and Michigan, met their targets for reading/language arts in the ELL subgroup (Zehr 2005). DOE researchers determined that many states were still developing their assessment databases to follow students over time or were changing assessments and could not submit data for the report. No state met targets for both reading and math with ELL students (Zehr 2005).

Urban Student Achievement

Urban schools frequently have high levels of poverty and minority subgroups. A study conducted by the Council of the Great City Schools, a Washington, D.C.–based advocacy group for sixty-five of the nation's largest urban districts, showed that the academic performance of students in ten cities improved in both reading and mathematics from 2001 to 2004. Fourth-graders improved more than 8th-graders. Fifty-five percent of the 4th grade met proficiency in math and 51 percent met proficiency in reading in 2004. Yet, only 44 percent of 8th-graders reached proficiency in math and 41 percent in reading.

In an effort to increase scores, Philadelphia schools reported using a new managed instruction program, teacher professional development, after school and summer school for struggling students, reading and math coaches, longer daily periods for core subjects, and formative assessment every six to ten weeks. Richmond schools provided mentors for teachers embedding assessment in daily instruction, after school, evenings, and Saturday tutoring. Other urban schools requested permission from the Education Department to use federal funds to run their own tutoring programs (Gewertz 2005, April 6).

Special Education Achievement

Most students with disabilities took state reading tests in 2003–2004. While complete data for state mathematics tests was not available, forty-one states reported that at least 95 percent of their students with disabilities took state exams. Few states reported using alternative tests because they found the time and expertise required to design these tests and provide training for teachers to implement them necessitated a longer period for development. Consequently, alternative tests were not available (Samuels 2005, August).

Under rules proposed for students with disabilities, separate assessments based on standards set to match abilities were allowed by the DOE. Students scoring as proficient on those tests could then be counted as proficient. Under this proposed rule, 2 percent of a school or district's enrollment could be tested against the modified standard. NCLB currently has a 1 percent cap for students with severe cognitive disabilities who take alternative below-grade-level tests. The new rule would require states to develop new standards and tests for academically challenged students. Controversy has surrounded the 1 percent rule because states find that 1 percent is too low. Advocacy groups argued that the new 2 percent rule would allow schools to retreat from policies forcing them to improve instruction (Hoff 2005, April 13).

For the 2005 school year, the secretary of education unveiled the 2 percent rule that permits eligible states to identify schools and districts that did not make accountability targets because of their special education population's low achievement scores. Using a proxy method, those states could increase the percentage of students with disabilities considered proficient by an equivalent of 2 percent of all students assessed. This flexibility has helped Florida, Georgia, and Virginia meet accountability targets this year. Some individuals are concerned that the DOE has set its estimates too high with the 2 percent rule. This formula could exclude as many as 30 percent of all special education students from having to meet grade-level standards (Olson 2005, September 21).

In 2005, two Illinois school districts sued the federal department and their state board of education, arguing that the NCLB law's requirement that special education students count as a subgroup for school accountability conflicts with the Individuals with Disabilities Education Act (IDEA) mandate that each student have an individual education plan. This suit is currently pending in the U.S. District Court in Chicago (Hendrie 2005, May 4).

Joint Test Development

Three small states, New Hampshire, Rhode Island, and Vermont, have collaborated to develop math and reading 3–8 tests for accountability.

They are currently jointly developing writing tests for grades five and eight. The states plan to set common performance standards and common ways to report results with testing that uses a short answer format. The greatest challenge for collaborative test development has been working out administrative procedures and the specific test design because the different state histories and state cultures must be considered. However, each state expects to save millions of dollars on this joint endeavor (Olson 2005, October 19).

SUMMARY AND CONCLUSIONS

The NCLB Act has forced the nation's schools to change how they conduct business. Accountability has shifted from state education departments to schools and even individuals. There is a major focus upon student achievement and consequently curriculum, instruction, and assessment. All fifty states now have an accountability system and are in varying stages of data collection and follow up. Although moderate, there appears to be evidence of increases in student achievement, particularly in math and reading. Subgroups such as English language learners, urban students, and students with disabilities are receiving increased attention and making small achievement gains.

Still, there is some evidence to suggest that many public schools may not have the internal capacity to effect sufficient change without additional support from the state and federal government. At the same time, there is a considerable outcry from other parent and education groups criticizing NCLB because of the emphasis on testing with a one-size-fits-all mentality. Thus, institutionalizing NCLB may require development of different kinds of policies and procedures than those now available at state and federal levels.

CHAPTER 1 REFLECTION QUESTIONS

1. Consider your school and district. How have accountability and assessment evolved over the last fifteen years? Ten years? Five years?

2. What changes have occurred in your school and district?

3. What negative and positive effects have occurred in your school and district?

4. How are different stakeholders in your school and district responding to this increased accountability?

5. Why do you think the states are so worried in their responses to NCLB?

CHAPTER 1 HELPFUL WEBSITES

Department of Education:
www.ed.gov/index.jhtml

Elementary and Secondary Education Act:
www.ed.gov/policy/elsec/leg/esea02/beginning.html#sec2

English Language Learners:
www.ed.gov/about/offices/list/oela/index.html

Goals 2000:
www.ed.gov/legislation/GOALS2000/TheAct/index.html

Nation at Risk:
www.ed.gov/pubs/NatAtRisk/risk.html

National Assessment of Educational Progress:
nces.ed.gov/nationsreportcard/

No Child Left Behind:
www.ed.gov/nclb/landing.jhtml

2

Adequate Yearly Progress (AYP)

At sea you can't control the winds, but you can control the sail.

—Roland Barth, educator and author

States must establish the definition of adequate yearly progress (AYP) that districts and schools are required to meet. Also, they must specify annual objectives to measure progress of districts and schools to ensure that all groups of students, including those with learning disabilities, low-income students, students from all racial and ethnic groups, and students with limited English proficiency reach state-specified levels of completion within twelve years. States must set intermediate benchmarks that provide AYP targets beginning in the 2004–2005 school year. In order to make AYP schools must test at least 95 percent of their students in each of the subpopulation groups listed above (U.S. Department of Education 2002).

The AYP aspect of NCLB has changed the way states evaluate schools, school districts, and even the states themselves. Not only is there an overall performance rating but the progress of every subgroup is examined. State criteria must be met in order for schools to receive an acceptable rating. States have approached AYP standards differently, but ultimately by 2014 all states must show that 100 percent of their students are proficient. The intent of NCLB is to ensure that every child learns and if a child does not learn, schools will be held accountable. A discussion of selected states' AYP proficiency increments follows.

STATE AYP PROFICIENCY INCREMENTS

Florida implemented the Florida comprehensive assessment test (FCAT) in January 1998 to measure student achievement in reading and math. The FCAT uses five achievement levels: Level 1 is below basic; Level 2 is basic; Levels 3 and 4 are proficient; and Level 5 is advanced. Students scoring a three (3) or above are considered proficient for the purpose of adequate yearly progress (AYP). While Florida boasts of gains in reading for fourth grade students and gains in achievement for minority students, the minority subgroups are still performing at lower levels than white students. For example, in 2004, 63 percent of white students were considered proficient, while 32 percent of African American students and 42 percent of Hispanic students were considered proficient.

Data also suggest that the number of Florida students who score at Level 1 continues to decline, while the number of students who are scoring at Level 3 or above continues to increase (Florida Department of Education 2004). Florida has set intermediate goals for reading and mathematics for all students across all grade levels in order to reach 100 percent proficiency by 2013–2014.

Florida responded to then Secretary of Education Margaret Spelling's announcement of flexible implementation of NCLB for states that show results and follow the principles of NCLB. As a result, the state has received permission to revise the annual targets for the percentage of students who must score at the proficient level or higher on reading and mathematics tests. Florida's new targets require at least 37 percent of the students to score at the proficient level in reading in 2004–2005 and 44 percent in math. These percentages are down from 48 percent in reading and 53 percent in math that were first set by the state. The result of this change means that the state will measure results in smaller annual percentage increments. However, the law that all students will be proficient by 2014 has not changed (Olson 2005, October 26).

Illinois used the percentage of proficient students in the 20th percentile to establish the starting point as 40 percent for reading. In 2005 and 2006 proficiency is 47.5 percent and continues to grow to 77.5 percent by 2010. In 2011, proficiency is determined by 85 percent, 92.5 percent by 2012, and finally, by 100 percent in 2014.

Illinois reported that 132 more schools and 100 more districts met the tough NCLB standards in 2004 than in 2003 (Illinois State Board of Education n.d.). The Illinois State Board of Education reported that 201 districts and 142 schools failed solely because of testing results reported for special education students. The State Board has stated that the current system for testing special education students does not adequately account for their unique needs.

Illinois cites another subgroup with unique characteristics, that of the limited English proficient (LEP) subgroup for bilingual students. This group of students, unlike any other subgroup, exits their subgroup two years after they become proficient in English. Illinois cites statistics that show that 69 percent of the districts that failed to make AYP did so because of low test results attributed to one or the other of these two subgroups (Illinois State Board of Education n.d.).

Utah has established an accountability system that utilizes a baseline. All student subgroups within the same grade levels use the same starting point and the same measurable objectives, which were designed to culminate in 100 percent proficiency by 2013–2014. The starting point for Language Arts grades three through eight is 65 percent and for Language Arts High School is 64 percent. The calculation of the annual measurable objective involves determining a weighted average of the percentage of proficient students at all grade levels in the school (Utah State Board of Education n.d.).

Utah has set a rigorous schedule of goals to meet the 2014 goal of 100 percent. However, data suggest that work is needed to close the achievement gap between minorities and white students. While slightly more than 80 percent of white students were rated as proficient on the Language Arts criterion referenced test (CRT), less than 50 percent of Hispanic students, 59 percent of black students, and 50 percent of American Indian students were rated as proficient (Utah State Board of Education n.d.).

Utah defines four proficiency levels for all core CRTs: Level 1, Minimal; Level 2, Partial; Level 3, Sufficient; Level 4, Substantial. Levels 1 and 2 correspond to the basic federal level, while Level 3 corresponds to the proficient, and Level 4 corresponds to the advanced federal level.

As the 2005 timeline for achieving student proficiency in core academic areas nears many states have requested federal flexibility in their state standards to enable more schools and districts to achieve AYP status. Growth models are one example of flexibility now being considered by the secretary of education.

AYP GROWTH MODELS

Federal officials are considering alternatives for measuring progress. Growth models give schools and districts credit for increasing student achievement even if they have not reached proficiency goals. Defining what is meant by growth and measuring it is far from clear. The Massachusetts model requires schools to meet the state's current AYP target for the total population and for each subgroup. Schools and subgroups below target make AYP if their rate of improvement based on the index where they started is steep enough that all students would reach proficiency by 2014.

Minnesota and Oklahoma use a safe harbor method to take a second look at schools not making AYP initially. Safe harbor permits them to make AYP if they reduce the percentage of nonproficient students in subgroups that missed the target by 10 percent from the previous year. Some feel that a 10 percent jump is unreasonable to expect for many schools.

Massachusetts and other states compare performance of different cohort groups over time to determine growth. Because a student body or profile of a grade level may vary each year, critics of the safe harbor method contend that comparisons over time are not equating the same groups. Additionally, such comparisons may identify characteristics of student populations rather than student achievement growth because test scores correlate with student characteristics such as poverty, gender, or ethnicity (Olson 2005, March 23).

The DOE convened a working group to consider adopting growth models in June 2005. Special educators are especially interested in the growth model. Yet, currently the NCLB law does not permit growth models except as a means of enhancing current AYP calculations (Olson 2005, July 13).

SUBGROUPS AND AYP CALCULATIONS

Subgroups for AYP purposes appear problematic. In order to make AYP under NCLB public schools and districts must meet annual state targets for the percentage of the students scoring at least proficient on state tests. All students must be considered to include the different subgroup populations.

According to a recent report in Education Week (Olson 2005, September 21), more than 80 percent of the schools making AYP targets in 2003–2004 did not have to meet standard proficiency for special education students as a separate subgroup because of the size of the threshold the states set before the subgroup needed to be calculated in their AYP.

The DOE permits states to set the minimum number that needs to be in a subgroup before that subgroup counts separately in determining the district or school AYP status. This provision was designed to avoid letting a small number of students skew the school's AYP status. Based on a study conducted by the National Center on Educational Outcomes at the University of Minnesota, as the number of students per subgroup approached sixty, all of the schools met their AYP targets without having to include the performance of special education students as a separate subgroup (Olson 2005, September 21).

Twenty-two states require subgroups to reach the size of forty before they calculate AYP. Oklahoma, West Virginia, and Wisconsin require a minimum of fifty students for subgroups. Ohio and Nebraska require their special education subgroups to have a larger number of students than their other subgroups (Olson 2005, September 21).

SPECIAL EDUCATION AND AYP

Including special education students in accountability system measures is controversial because by definition, special education students have disabilities that interfere with learning. Historically, special education students in general perform at much lower levels on state tests. *Education Week* (Olson 2005, September 21) gathered information substantiating the effect of subgrouping special education students.

For example, West Virginia with a subgroup of 50 included 715 of their schools in accountability ratings in 2005 but only 146, or 20 percent, had to meet separate subgroups targets for students with disabilities. California with a total of 9,188 schools had only 699, or 8 percent, required to meet AYP targets in reading and math for special education. Over one-half of the California schools missing AYP targets in 2005 did so because of special education.

Florida raised their subgroup for AYP to thirty, or 15 percent, of the student population. Forty-two percent of the Florida schools did not meet AYP targets because of special education. Georgia has adjusted their subgroup numbers to forty, or 10 percent, of the student population (Olson 2005, September 21).

NEW RULES FOR SPECIAL EDUCATION

The Department of Education has allowed some test flexibility for states in 2005 only. States may use this flexibility option if they have a 95 percent or more test participation rate and they use the same subgroup size for students with disabilities as they use for other subgroups. States may use a mathematical formula to increase the passing rate for students with disabilities or the state may count more scores from alternative tests as proficient (Samuels 2005, May 18).

The 2003 federal regulations permitted states to develop alternative achievement standards to measure the progress of students with significant cognitive disabilities. One percent of the scores were considered proficient. Teachers, schools, and states complained that the 1 percent rule did not address student progress for those having moderate disabilities that could not attain grade-level proficiency.

In May 2005, the Department of Education unveiled the 2 percent rule (Olson 2005, September 21). For 2005 only eligible states were permitted to identify schools or districts that did not attain AYP because of special education and count as proficient up to 2 percent of all students assessed. This rule has made a significant difference in the number of schools meeting AYP targets. In Florida an additional 150 schools met AYP. In Virginia 54 additional schools met AYP targets and in Georgia 69 more met AYP (Olson 2005, September 21). Advocacy groups and individuals have expressed concern that the 2 percent rule estimates are too high because the proportion of students not expected to perform at grade level excludes about 30 percent of all special education (Olson 2005, September 21).

STATES REPORT AYP—2005

By August 2005, thirty-three states and the District of Columbia had submitted AYP reports. About half showed the number of schools meeting AYP increased while the other half indicated decreasing numbers of schools meeting AYP targets. Major differences occurred in the way AYP proficiency was calculated. For example, some states raised the minimum subgroup size. Georgia raised minimum subgroup size for all subgroups, while Minnesota raised the subgroup size from twenty to forty for LEP students. Mississippi and Wisconsin used a 99 percent confidence interval to calculate AYP. Minnesota averages proficiency rates over a two-year period. Several states, such as Oregon and Maryland, identify districts for improvement only if they do not meet AYP in the same subject for two consecutive years. Idaho and Tennessee adjusted the percentage of proficient students with disabilities in schools based on their special education subgroup using the 2 percent rule (Olson 2005, September 7).

The Education Department has granted flexibility to sixteen different states (Olson 2005, July 13). An example of state flexibility in AYP calculation is provided in table 2.1.

Table 2.1 reports AYP information for 2005 from the selected states. Education Week Research Center data reported by Olson (2005, September 7) showed that of the seven states, five made AYP standards. Once again, there is a wide variance in the different states. The states not sending data were in the process of establishing a database at the time the report was written.

All states must include Title I schools in their designations of schools in need of improvement. Federal law allows states to choose whether non-Title I schools are assigned a school improvement status and whether consequences apply to those schools. As a result, some schools rated for AYP may not receive a school improvement designation. The percentages reported in table 2.1 were calculated by dividing the total number of schools identified as in need of improvement by the total number of schools rated for AYP (Olson 2005, September 7, p. 27).

Table 2.1.   AYP Progress—Selected States 2005

State	Percentage of Schools Meeting AYP	Percentage of Schools Identified in Need of Improvement	Percentage of Students At or Above Proficient Level			
			4th Grade Reading	8th Grade Reading	4th Grade Math	8th Grade Math
California	56	Sept. 05	47	39	50	37[a]
Connecticut	82	15[b]	67	75	79	76
Kentucky	74	11	68	62[a]	45[a]	36
New York	Sept. 05	Sept. 05	70	48	—	—
Texas	87	3	79	83	81	61
Utah	Oct. 05	Oct. 05	Oct. 05	Oct. 05	Oct. 05	Oct. 05
Virginia	81	6	77[a]	76	88[a]	81

Notes:
a. State did not administer tests at grades 4 or 8. Test results accepted from next closest grade level.
b. Connecticut reported results for only elementary and middle schools. High school information not reported.

Source: L. Olson, "NCLB Continues to Challenge Schools in 2005," *Education Week* 25, no. 2 (2005, September 7): 27.

SUMMARY AND CONCLUSIONS

Achievement testing has been around for a long time. With Goals 2000 a number of states developed achievement tests for reading and math as part of their effective schools' accountability systems. Title I programs have always required academic tests for placement and to examine student progress. What is different under NCLB is that schools are required to assess student achievement and set state standards for academic proficiency and they are being held accountable for results for all subgroups of students. Flexibility in the form of innovative approaches for counting students from subgroup populations, particularly special education, has emerged so that schools will not be punished because a few students were unable to meet grade-level expectations. Sixteen states have been granted flexibility for 2005 allowing a significant number of schools to meet AYP that would not meet state standards because of special education. Of the seven states examined, percentages of schools reaching AYP standards varied from a low of 56 percent in California to a high of 87 percent in Texas. Some states did not report AYP information because they are still developing databases. It is impossible to directly compare AYP across states because of the differences in assessment types, AYP calculations, and in state-set AYP standards.

There is no research that supports the premise that all students and all subgroups of students can reach meaningful high standards by 2014 as required by NCLB. Given the lack of social, economic, and family assets of many students and the capacity for schools or states to provide sufficient support, AYP sanctions appear both negative and unrealistic.

A key element of the NCLB Act is the requirement for all Title I classrooms to have a highly qualified teacher. A discussion of this element follows.

CHAPTER 2 REFLECTION QUESTIONS

1. How has AYP affected your school and district?

2. Evaluate your school's and your district's subgroup data.

3. Using your school's and your district's data, what subgroups are in need of extra support?

4. What support is being provided for teachers of these subgroups?

5. What support is being provided for students of these subgroups?

6. What strategies would you recommend that your school and district have not yet implemented?

CHAPTER 2 HELPFUL WEBSITES

California Department of Education:
  www.cde.ca.gov/

Florida Comprehensive Assessment Test:
  www.firn.edu/doe/sas/fcat.htm

Highly Qualified Teachers:
  www.ed.gov/nclb/methods/teachers/hqtflexibility.html

Illinois State Board of Education:
  www.isbe.state.il.us/

National Center on Educational Outcomes at the University of Minnesota:
  education.umn.edu/NCEO/

Texas Education Agency:
  www.tea.state.tx.us/

State of Utah Office of Education:
  www.usoe.k12.ut.us/

3

Highly Qualified Teachers

Good teachers put snags in the river of children passing by, and over the years, they redirect hundreds of lives.

—Tracy Kidder, Pulitzer Prize–winning author

DEFINITION AND STATUS

To satisfy the highly qualified standard of NCLB, each teacher of a core subject must hold a bachelor's degree and a state standard teaching credential, as well as demonstrate knowledge of the subject taught. New teachers become highly qualified by taking and passing tests in the subjects they teach or completing the equivalent of a college major. Veteran teachers may choose to meet highly qualified requirements through alternative evaluations that include consideration for years of experience and professional development.

States continue to report that the majority of their core academic classes are taught by teachers deemed highly qualified. Several states, including California, Delaware, Hawaii, Maryland, Nevada, New Hampshire, New Mexico, and Utah, reported that more than 25 percent of their courses were taught by teachers not considered highly qualified (Olson 2005, March 16).

Highly Qualified

By the end of the 2005–2006 school year states are required to stop granting waivers of their teacher certification requirements of NCLB. In 2003–
2004 *Education Week* (2005, October 5, p. 13) reported that 3.5 percent of
the nation's core-subject teachers held waivers. The comparable figure for
high-poverty districts was 5.2 percent.

A number of states are not able to meet the NCLB mandate that a highly
qualified teacher is assigned to every classroom by the end of the 2005–
2006 year. California appears in desperate straits to meet this mandate citing class size reduction mandates and teacher retirements. Florida cites
similar problems along with rapidly increasing student enrollments. Consequently, the Secretary of Education has granted a one-year waiver to
states for complying with the highly qualified requirement if they map out
plans for compliance and get approval from federal officials. At the same
time, the Education Department has begun verifying teacher-quality information from states. Under NCLB, states are required to ensure that
school districts provide information to parents about the highly qualified
status of teachers to include the percentage placed in high-poverty schools
(Keller 2005, November 2).

HOUSSE Rules

Thirty states have developed point systems through high, objective, uniform state standard of evaluation (HOUSSE) rules to assist veteran
teachers. California has been criticized for leniency in letting teachers
earn points toward highly qualified status for such activities as leadership
and service roles over the course of their careers. Florida's HOUSSE system requires teachers to pass a subject-matter evaluation which appears
to be a one-shot annual observation by the principal. Florida's plan includes successful teaching experience, principal's evaluations, and professional development. HOUSSE rules have been criticized because they
side-step NCLB requirements for solid content-area preparation (Sack
2005, November).

HIGHLY QUALIFIED FOR SPECIAL EDUCATION

Achieving highly qualified status in subject areas has caused more confusion than clarity for special education teachers. Reauthorization of the Individuals with Disabilities Education Act (IDEA) prescribed laws for educating some 6.5 million students with disabilities. With the November, 2005 reauthorization of IDEA legislators attempted to align special education laws with those of the No Child Left Behind Act, which spells out accountability requirement for all public schools. NCLB mandates ensure that teachers are highly qualified, thus reauthorization of IDEA required that special education teachers must meet the same standards of quality as teachers of general education by the end of the 2005–2006 school year. This means that special education teachers must be highly qualified in special education as well as every subject they teach (Samuels 2005, February 16, p. 22).

Many special education teachers have years of experience teaching a variety of content areas. Such teachers could have a bachelor's degree in elementary education and a master's degree in special education or vice versa. Yet, if they do not have a content area specialty they are not considered highly qualified under NCLB.

For veteran teachers HOUSSE evaluation standards differ from state to state and allow loopholes through which teachers not having sufficient content credit may use experience, professional development and classroom information to obtain highly qualified status. Special education teachers must rely heavily on HOUSSE evaluations. Professional organizations, federal and state education professionals, and university preparation programs are examining certification requirements for special educators so that changes may occur before the NCLB reauthorization in 2007. Not all states have a HOUSSE evaluation in place causing extreme anxiety for special education teachers in those states.

California is one of thirty states with a menu system for HOUSSE. In California, years of teaching experience, professional development, school leadership, classroom observation, and evaluation of lesson plans are assigned point values. For example, experience counts up to 50 points and 20 clock hours of professional development counts 5 points. A teacher must accumulate 100 points to be highly qualified. Kansas has written a standard to be used for teachers who instruct multiple subjects. Some special educators have expressed concern that the highly qualified standards stress academic content at the expense of pedagogy. For special educators, knowing how to deal with challenging students may be as important as content knowledge (Samuels 2005, February 16, p. 22).

PREPARATION FOR HIGHLY QUALIFIED TEACHERS

The NCLB requirement for highly qualified teachers has stirred a debate over teacher preparation. Traditionally, Americans believed that knowing how to teach was as important as knowing what to teach. A fundamental disagreement now exists over whether traditional teacher preparation or content area preparation has more influence on student achievement. Darling-Hammond (2001) found that teacher preparation correlates more strongly with student achievement than class size, overall spending or teacher salaries, and accounts for 40–60 percent of the total achievement variance after consideration of student demographics. Both pedagogy and content knowledge were found to strongly correlate with teacher classroom performance.

Rod Paige (2002) in his annual report on teacher quality, found no scientifically rigorous research to support the belief that pedagogy or education degrees are linked to higher student achievement. Using such logic, NCLB legislation removed teacher preparation in educational theory and practice and allowed content area expertise to take precedence for teachers at the middle and high school levels.

Research connecting teacher certification and teacher quality appears mixed. Teacher certification standards vary from state to state. If teacher candidates have content knowledge linked to pedagogy and integrate this with students in a supervised setting, certification could be a strong predictor of teacher quality (Kaplan and Owing, 2003).

However, Houston (2005) suggests that highly qualified does not necessarily mean good teachers. It means they took the right courses in college to match the content they are assigned to teach. Houston also points out that private schools have made their reputations using uncertified teachers and sometimes non-approved curriculum. Public school information is open to scrutiny on a daily basis and that alone should be considered accountability.

The highly qualified requirement for teachers has impacted university preparation programs. Universities will have to examine their preparation programs in tandem with state certification requirements. For example, meeting the highly qualified content area standard in Ohio requires forty-five hours of training in each subject (Samuels 2005, February 16).

PLACEMENTS FOR HIGHLY QUALIFIED TEACHERS

Disparities still exist in placements of highly qualified and experienced teachers. Placements most likely to have inexperienced and uncertified teachers appear to be in 9th grade and in high-poverty schools. Black, Hispanic, and low-achieving students tended to have disproportionately high numbers of uncertified and new teachers. Virginia is piloting teacher bonuses as a means of attracting high-quality teachers for hard-to-staff schools and to attract highly qualified math teachers.

Table 3.1 provides an example of selected states' highly qualified teacher placements by percentage for all districts and high-poverty districts. Only Virginia reported that all teachers were highly qualified. The overall trend supports allegations that high-poverty districts have fewer highly qualified teacher placements than more affluent districts.

Viadero (2005, April 20) suggests that freshman students in urban high schools were less likely than their older peers to get certified and experienced teachers. Results of a study conducted in 1999–2000 found the

Table 3.1.   Placement of Teachers Who Are Not Highly Qualified

State	All Districts (Percentage)	High-poverty Districts (Percentage)
California	5.6	6.3
Connecticut	1.4	1.8
Kentucky	4.1	3.4
New York	0.6	1.7
Texas	7.8	8.3
Utah	4.5	7.0
Virginia	0.0	0.0

Source: USDOE Higher Education Act, Title II, 2004; *Education Week* 25, no. 8: 13.

overall percentages of new or uncertified teachers ranged from 8 percent to 60 percent in thirty-five high schools tracked (Viadero 2005, April 20). Magnet and vocational schools had the fewest uncertified teachers. Black, Hispanic, and low-achieving students tended to get disproportionately high numbers of new and uncertified teachers (Viadero 2005, April 20).

HIGHLY QUALIFIED TEACHERS FOR HARD-TO-STAFF SCHOOLS

Representatives of three education organizations have formed a partnership to focus attention on hiring and retaining high-quality teachers for hard-to-staff schools. The governor of Virginia stated that American education provided a perverse, reverse incentive system that pays teachers more and provides a better work environment in affluent neighborhoods but students in poor communities need highly qualified teachers more. The National Partnership for Teaching in At-Risk Schools published a report citing studies that showed that inexperienced teachers were more likely to teach in high-poverty schools. High-poverty schools traditionally had far fewer teachers with subject-area expertise.

Virginia is currently piloting an incentives pay program that offered experienced teachers, with at least five years' experience and a record of addressing student achievement, hiring bonuses of $15,000. These teachers must stay in hard-to-staff schools for three years. Additionally, teachers in the pilot districts who have five years' experience and academic degrees in the subject areas they teach receive annual $3,000 bonuses for staying. The schools earn extra state money if students reach state-set proficiency goals. Preliminary results of the pilot suggest that the program is bolstering teacher morale (Richard 2005, February 16, p. 5).

A second Virginia incentives program provides bonuses for highly qualified math teachers. Based on this initiative the state will compile a list of math experts for schools to hire. The purpose of the program was to assist seventy middle schools designated as low-performing in math. Teachers must have at least three years of experience teaching math, a college major or minor in math, and a state teaching credential for middle school level math. These teachers may be paid as much as $10,000 for each year of their three-year commitment. Districts and schools are required to apply for the bonus money by developing a plan showing how they would use these teachers based on the school's math-achievement deficiencies (Keller 2005).

PROFESSIONAL DEVELOPMENT
FOR HIGHLY QUALIFIED TEACHERS

National policy makers believe that professional development can be an important factor in improving student achievement. The NCLB Act reflected this belief by allocating 2.9 billion dollars in 2005 for use in professional development activities, class-size reduction, or other initiatives aimed at the improvement of teacher quality (Viadero 2005, July 27).

Professional development is a form of adult learning. Yet schools often forget that under NCLB, high-quality professional development must primarily address student learning. Just attending workshops or conferences or working on curriculum during workshop days has not proved to be particularly effective in raising student achievement. Currently, school reform efforts have identified processes enhancing teacher collaboration and communication as effective tools for teacher professional development (Kelleher 2003).

Innovative Approaches to Professional Development

NCLB supports long-term intensive professional development focusing upon academic contents teachers must cover in their classes. A number of innovative professional development approaches are emerging. Teachers have found peer support and working in small groups at grade level or with like-content teachers beneficial in being able to discuss issues and applications that enhance students' learning and retention. Learning coaches assigned to one or a group of teachers appear helpful by providing content or pedagogy expertise or for modeling and classroom demonstrations, although research on the effectiveness of such approaches for adult learning is inconclusive (Viadero 2005, July 27).

Florida and Utah are using literacy coaches to assist both new and veteran teachers with lessons, improve teaching strategies, select materials, analyze student data, and find relevant research articles. Some coaches' positions have been established with federal Reading First grants, but some employed in elementary, middle, and high schools are not receiving federal aid. Because schools have realized that reading achievement hinges on the knowledge and skill of teachers, schools have invested monetary resources in the continuing support and professional development that coaches can offer.

As the popularity of coaches has grown, so have concerns about the qualifications of those hired to coach. Reading coaching is not just teaching reading; it entails working with adults to support their growth, developing trust, and providing job-embedded context for professional development (Manzo 2005, July 27).

Boston uses literacy coaches to work at least once per week in each K–12 school. Study teams at each school work with an assigned coach to study student data. The teams read professional articles on a topic, discuss findings, and prepare lesson plans for the coach to demonstrate and then try in different teacher participants' classrooms. Literacy coaches are expected to understand adult learners and it is their job to facilitate teacher learning, provide information, and literacy content to assist teachers (Manzo 2005, July 27).

Teacher Learning Groups

In 1995, the Massachusetts Department of Education provided funds to 350 districts to create teacher study groups. Facilitators were provided training to conduct the groups. Study groups were encouraged because of the learning teachers obtained through peer dialogue concerning teaching and student learning. Study groups were encouraged to send in products of their work, such as videotapes of lessons being taught, curriculum units integrating standards, and lesson plans. Participants provided testimonials that the study group forum was a safe place to take risks and talk about their practices (French 1998).

Similarly, a lesson study model has been recommended as a vehicle to foster in-depth examination of the teaching process. The lesson study model encouraged a small group of teachers to collaborate, using a recursive cycle of articulating a clear lesson plan, observing the teaching of this lesson, and then discussing and revising the plan and instruction if deemed necessary. The process of developing a detailed lesson plan, then discussing it with colleagues, proved to be a powerful tool for instructional improvement. Administrative support for this type of professional development is necessary to allow teachers time to videotape, develop, plan, reflect, and modify teaching practices (Stewart and Brendefur 2005).

Walk-through Initiative

Seven Louisiana districts are trying to transform classroom visits from observations of teacher behavior to observations of student behavior based on the New York City system, community School District 2, which pioneered walk-throughs in the 1980s. The Louisiana effort was initiated with a U.S. Department of Education grant. Principals who volunteered to participate did not know how to analyze instruction because traditionally that skill was not a focus of their preparation. Teacher perceptions are crucial to the success of walk-through initiatives. Some educators have suggested that classroom visits focusing on what students are learning provides a powerful learning tool for teachers. The Louisiana endeavor is still a work in progress (Archer 2005, July 27).

SUMMARY AND CONCLUSIONS

Under NCLB, highly qualified status is tied to state teacher certification or licensure and demonstrated teachers' impact on student learning. Professional development has been linked to increasing student achievement, although research does not clearly establish such a link. The NCLB Act supports professional development through innovative initiatives, and new staff development strategies are emerging.

Learning or literacy coaches appear popular, but evidence of effectiveness is not sufficient because such programs are new and evaluation data are not available. Concerns about the training and qualifications of coaches have surfaced and training has been recommended, particularly in the area of adult learning and developing relationships. Louisiana is piloting a classroom visit initiative. Classroom walk-throughs are not new. Walk-throughs must be handled with extreme care because teachers are super sensitive concerning perceived evaluation of their behavior or practices. Collaborative teacher learning groups appear to have more potential as professional development strategies than traditional professional development workshops. Principals must have training in observing curriculum and instruction practices in classroom observations relative to student learning since that has not been part of their preparation.

In conclusion, teacher certification does not ensure teacher quality and vice versa. There is insufficient evidence to suggest that content knowledge alone will guarantee teacher effectiveness. Yet, regardless of certification or teacher preparation, effective teachers can affect student achievement. Highly qualified teachers are critical to effectively navigate the waters of NCLB.

CHAPTER 3 REFLECTION QUESTIONS

1. Describe the impact of highly qualified teachers on your school and district.

2. Study the data on your school and district for highly qualified. Summarize your school's and your district's status.

3. What programs are your school and district providing now to see that teachers attain this status?

4. What programs can your school and district implement in the future to help teachers become highly qualified?

5. What resources do your school and your district need to adequately prepare teachers?

6. Do you think there is a connection between National Board Certified Teachers and highly qualified?

CHAPTER 3 HELPFUL WEBSITES

Adult Learning:
   honolulu.hawaii.edu/intranet/committees/FacDevCom/guidebk/
    teachtip/adults-2.htm

HOUSSE Rules:
   doe.sd.gov/educationonline/2005/november/art_article1.asp

Individuals with Disabilities Education Act:
   www.ed.gov/offices/OSERS/Policy/IDEA/index.html

Literacy Coaches:
   www.carnegie.org/reporter/09/literacy/index.html

Magnet Schools:
   www.magnet.edu/

Massachusetts Department of Education:
   www.doe.mass.edu/

National Partnership for Teaching in At-Risk Schools:
   www.ncrel.org/quality/partnership.htm

Reauthorization of IDEA (December 2004):
   www.wrightslaw.com/news/idea2002.htm

Vocational Schools:
   www.rwm.org/rwm/

4

Title I: Overview

Rivers are roads which move and which carry us where we desire to go.

—Blaise Pascal, philosopher

POVERTY AND ECONOMIC FACTORS

Poverty has not been considered a problem of American economic organization, but one of individual or group characteristics. Under Presidents Kennedy and Johnson in the 1960s, the war on poverty offered training programs that focused on high crime rates, ignorance, apathy, and lack of positive role models. Federal initiatives focused on training and employment programs. When employment became stagnant as it did in the 1970s, many training program participants lost interest in pursuing training for positions when there was little chance of employment. Since that time there has been a sharp increase in urban poverty, joblessness, minority female-headed families, homelessness, and welfare dependency (Yudof, Kirp, Levin, and Moran 2002).

Yudof and colleagues (2002) suggest that changes in the U.S. poverty rate are tied to changes in economic performance. A one percent increase in the general base level unemployment level, for example the unemployment level for white males, generates 2 percent to 2.5 percent unemployment levels for poverty groups consisting of black males, minority female heads of households, elderly, and other entry-level employees who are hard hit when unemployment rises and real income declines. Additionally, the effectiveness of training programs, education programs, and employment programs depend upon a favorable economic climate (Yudof et al. 2002).

TITLE I: HISTORICAL BACKGROUND

Although state governments have the primary responsibility for elementary and secondary public education, the federal government has provided limited but significant support for students from poverty backgrounds. Title I of the Elementary and Secondary Education Act (ESEA) of 1965 has emerged as the embodiment of the federal commitment to assist with educating economically and educationally disadvantaged children. Title I legislation has been reauthorized every five years over the past four decades (Jennings 2000).

Most of President Kennedy's legislative proposals for education were not enacted. States feared a larger federal role in education; the South feared desegregation; Catholic schools and other private schools blocked legislation not favorable to them. President Lyndon Johnson tied education to the war on poverty that targeted federal assistance to categories of need. The ESEA Title I Program of 1965 provided aid to disadvantaged children and supported other categorical programs for the purchase of library books, created supplemental education centers, and supported the development of state departments of education. Title I funds would follow the eligible child and be administered through a public trustee, the school system (Jennings 2000).

From the initiation of Title I, the program exhibited difficulties as well as the potential for more and more federal control. A major question emerged concerning the purpose of the program. Was this program designed as supplementary education for disadvantaged students or as a major benefit for school systems, using the number of disadvantaged students to generate funding support? Once the program was implemented, $1 billion flowed to states and school districts. Confusion in implementing Title I resulted because of the confusing purpose (Jennings 2000; Yudof et al. 2002).

In 1969, a report based on Title I audits conducted by the Department of Health, Education and Welfare suggested that program funds were being used by schools to benefit all students, not just the disadvantaged, and for school administration support. This report resulted in the "supplement not supplant" requirement, which meant that services funded with federal dollars could not be provided in lieu of educational services disadvantaged children would have received from state and local dollars in absence of the supplementary federal dollars.

Reports of Title I mismanagement spawned stricter enforcement of federal bookkeeping concerning compliance devised to ensure funds were concentrated on the disadvantaged. As a result, there were regulations concerning administrative accountability, parental involvement, maximizing local discretion, and compliance through litigation designed to ensure specific objectives.

By 1980, Title I served millions of children across the nation, particularly children in the primary grades. Researchers noted that Title I schools had made significant progress in decreasing inequalities between minority and nonminority students. Title I marked a shift in public policy because it changed what society expected of public schools and what the more disadvantaged society expected for itself (Jennings 2000).

Early Implementation of Title I

During the 1980s and early 1990s, disadvantaged children were often pulled out of the regular classroom for supplementary assistance through Title I reading and math programs. Parents and local community individuals were often hired as Title I aides to work with children. There was a belief that pull-out programs provided disadvantaged children more individualized assistance (Yudof et al. 2002).

Yudof and colleagues (2002) suggest that on the average, pull-out programs only added an additional ten minutes a day of extra instruction. These programs had little effect on regular instruction, where disadvantaged students spent the major part of their school day. Pull-out programs came with a high price tag for children missing instruction in the regular classroom in the core subjects of reading and math. Generally, using pull-out programs it was easier to document compliance. School administrators often complained about being overburdened by paperwork requirements for compliance. Consequently, significant drawbacks of pull-out programs included missed instruction in the regular classroom in favor of supplementary services under Title I (Jennings 2000).

Reagan-omics

The size and scope of Title I made it a prime target for the Reagan administration. Reagan did not succeed in eliminating Title I, but he was able to significantly cut back on expenditures for the program and curtail increased appropriations. The erosion for support for Title I in the early 1980s was so significant that it took ten years before the level of services was restored to that of 1980. Fewer children were served through Title I during the decade of the 1980s and federal aid to school districts became less significant. Title I became an add-on to regular instruction provided in the general classroom. Title I–funded aides and pull-out programs were still evident for fiscal accountability (Jennings 2000; Yudof et al. 2002).

The release of the Nation at Risk Report in 1983 had a significant impact on the general public and upon President Reagan. The perceived decline of the American economy was linked to the perceived failure of the public schools to raise student academic achievement. Further, the jobs of teachers, administrators, and even parents were complicated by the absence of clear Title I goals to serve as a framework to guide implementation. Thus, the program was driven by federally mandated achievement tests and minimum achievement results (Yudof et al. 2002).

The 1988 reauthorization of Title I required states to identify schools that did not show progress toward meeting achievement outcomes and to define levels of achievement that disadvantaged students should attain in schools receiving Title I funds. This focus on student achievement was a new experience for states, and state expectations varied.

Additionally, the law identified processes for districts and states to follow to assist low-performing schools. This was the first time school improvement plans were required and there were consequences spelled out for low-performing Title I schools. The 1988 statute also allowed some program flexibility in the form of schoolwide projects so that Title I funds could be used schoolwide if 75 percent of the students were considered disadvantaged (Jennings 2000).

Goals 2000 and the Clinton Administration—A New Title I Program

In 1994, Congress passed the Goals 2000 bill, which provided a philosophy for the reauthorization of the new Title I program. A major policy shift emphasized student outcomes—not inputs such as the amount of funds expended. Schools were required to set high achievement standards for all students and to develop and use achievement assessments. The eligibility threshold enabling schools to qualify for schoolwide Title I programs was lowered from 75 percent to 50 percent. States were given five years to implement the educational program under Goals 2000. Title I was the largest federal education program funded at $6.7 billion in 1994–1995 and it is still only one of many federal, state, and local programs serving disadvantaged students (Jennings 2000; Yudof et al. 2002).

NCLB 2001: Title I Reauthorized

In 2001, Title I was reauthorized as part of President George W. Bush's No Child Left Behind (NCLB) Act. Title I is the largest federal program supporting elementary and secondary education, funded at $10.4 billion in 2002. Title I targets those resources to districts and schools showing the greatest need. Schools with poverty rates of 50 percent or higher received 73 percent of Title I funds in 1997–1998, and nearly 96 percent of the highest poverty schools with 75 percent or more low-income students received Title I funds.

Title I focuses on promoting schoolwide reform in high-poverty schools and ensuring students' access to scientifically based instructional strategies and challenging academic content. Title I provisions include a mechanism for holding states, school districts, and schools accountable for improving the academic achievement of all students and turning around low-performing schools, while providing alternatives to students in such schools to enable those students to receive a high-quality education (U.S. Department of Education 2002, p. 13).

TITLE I: NEW ROLES AND NEW OPPORTUNITIES

School Level

Schools have become the centerpiece of Title I. School personnel are expected to become active participants in Title I programs and have greater authority to make program decisions. In the past, school planning was a rubber stamp for required documentation. However, the NCLB Title I program requires unprecedented, real collaboration to marshal and integrate the school's resources.

Principals will need to refocus their leadership efforts to include more emphasis on curriculum and instruction decision making. Teachers will need to make a concerted effort for real peer collaboration, partnerships, and sharing their expertise with colleagues to improve program planning, outcomes, and decision making. Parents will need real encouragement and assistance from school personnel to enable them to assume responsibility for sustaining ongoing dialogue concerning their children's educational needs (U.S. Department of Education 2002; Yudof et al. 2002).

District Level

School districts are expected to take on a support role in implementing Title I at the school level by providing technical assistance. Such assistance could include provision of district-level expertise for planning and program development or by providing an opportunity for school-level educators to observe what works in other districts or by connecting them with other technical assistance providers in universities or service centers. Districts are expected to assist schools in providing meaningful professional development connected to program goals and objectives.

Additionally, under the new Title I law, school districts are expected to assist with coordinating community partnerships and partnerships with other agencies and service providers. And last but not least, districts are expected to accept responsibility for providing oversight for low-performing schools to ensure support for required remedial actions and assuming a supportive facilitative stance (U.S. Department of Education 2002; Yudof et al. 2002).

State Department Level

NCLB has outlined specific duties and states are expected to create high-quality state standards and assessments and to align these components to ensure student success. States are also expected to have high expectations and to approve the use of any district-adopted standards and assessments used for Title I programs (U.S. Department of Education 2002; Yudof et al. 2002).

Federal Level

The new NCLB Title I is designed to focus on assistance rather than on control and compliance. Fifteen comprehensive technical centers were being developed to provide categorical assistance to states, districts, and schools to engage in schoolwide reform efforts. The federal plan is to focus on quality and results by moving programmatic decisions to states, districts, and schools with less control at the federal level and more local control to reflect state and local responsibility (Yudof et al. 2002).

CLOSING THE ACHIEVEMENT GAP

A major goal of Title I is to provide a means to close the achievement gaps found between disadvantaged and minority students and nondisadvantaged students. Some authors suggest that the rate of vocabulary growth at age three predicted measures of language skill at age nine or ten and these early vocabulary differences translated into the occurrence of reading readiness gaps emerging even before pre-K–12 schooling begins (Hart and Risley 1995).

A group of researchers analyzed longitudinal data from the Minnesota Comprehensive Assessment program to suggest that even the smallest one-point achievement gaps did not disappear in two years. The sample included 47,361 students who took the 3rd-grade math test and the 5th-grade math test two years later. Sampling error was negligible due to the large sample.

Researchers suggested that if the disadvantaged students versus nondisadvantaged students mean difference of 6.9 points was to be closed, then the disadvantaged students would need to make more progress than their nondisadvantaged peers. Analysis of the longitudinal data showed that the disadvantaged students made less progress than nondisadvantaged students when the scores were matched on third-grade achievement.

The MCA study found that once achievement gaps between student groups emerged, they tended to be persistent over time. These researchers

suggested that additional instructional time may be a crucial factor in closing achievement gaps. Three requirements of NCLB—high expectations
for all students, highly qualified teachers, and supplemental services—
were supported by the researchers for closing achievement gaps (Davison,
Young, Davenport Jr., Butterbaugh, and Davison 2004).

Ferguson and Mehta (2004) suggest that the National Assessment of Educational Progress (NAEP) continues to show large achievement gaps between races. They suggest that the Title I reauthorization, passed in 1994,
encouraged whole-school reforms in high-poverty schools and increased
the emphasis on accountability. However, the authors point out that results
of two large-scale program evaluations did not show Title I success in
closing the achievement gap between disadvantaged and nondisadvantaged students and the Head Start Program failed to show lasting results.

Ferguson and Mehta (2004) voiced concern that "achievement disparities among today's students foreshadow socioeconomic disparities among
tomorrow's families" (p. 667). They remain optimistic about the potential
offered through the new Title I law to close achievement gaps and en-
courage a research focus on what works. At the same time, they suggest a
need to go behind closed classroom doors and foster high-quality instructional practices for all children.

Improvement Plan

If a school fails to make adequate yearly progress for a third year, students
from low-income families must be given the option to use Title I funds to
obtain supplemental educational services from a public or private sector
provider, including faith-based organizations selected from a list of
providers approved by the state (U.S. Department of Education 2002).

Supplemental Education Services: Tutoring

Tutoring programs are the major focus of the Supplemental Education
Services (SES) mandated by the NCLB Act. Under the law, schools that
fail to make adequate yearly progress (AYP) and are considered to be in
need of improvement must offer eligible parents a choice of changing
schools or receiving free after-school tutoring services (U.S. Department
of Education 2002). Private after-school tutoring in America is a growing

business. As of 2002, annual expenditures for tutoring programs were estimated to be more than $5 billion and teachers were found to tutor more students (30 percent) than any other group whether community, nonprofit volunteers, peer tutors, or franchised tutoring centers (Gordon 2003).

The purpose of tutoring programs is to bridge achievement gaps between students from low socioeconomic backgrounds and other students. Public schools receiving Title I funds that are low-performing are a major focus for SES tutoring services. However, under the law, the Department of Education has not allowed districts in need of improvement to use Title I funds to provide tutoring services (Gewertz 2005, June 22). These districts have had to use their Title I funds to contract with outside agencies to provide tutoring. (See the discussion "Schools Seek Tutoring Waivers," below.)

Agencies providing tutor services include private schools, charter schools, community organizations, businesses, and faith-based organizations. Many companies and schools have endeavored to provide creative and innovative tutoring programs for at-risk students. There is some evidence of the U.S. Department of Education softening its policy toward public school districts providing their own tutoring programs with the release of waivers to some large urban districts to enable them to use Title I funds for tutoring even though they have not met their performance goals (Gewertz 2005, November 16).

Two organizations investigated the effectiveness of tutoring programs and cited several major concerns. There seemed to be a preponderance of programs, creating competition with existing programs. Some price gouging was noted by independent providers to be sure to use the full amount of funds allocated. There was a lack of Internet access by low-income families whose children needed tutoring. There was a lack of student attendance in tutoring programs in general and there was a lack of district or agency oversight to monitor tutoring program success (ACORN 2004).

Further, Wasik (1997) found little evidence documenting the effectiveness of using volunteers as tutors, and the cost of certified teachers serving as tutors was prohibitive. Effective reading programs that used paraprofessionals provided a highly structured program with tutor manuals, student materials, and training procedures (Wasik 1997). The Center for Education Policy found that only about 18 percent of all eligible students nationally received free tutoring in 2004–2005 (Richard 2005, December 7).

Rural District Tutoring

The U.S. Department of Education estimated that about 23 percent of the two million students qualifying for free tutoring received it in 2003–2004. Less populated states such as Montana, Wyoming, and South Dakota have few supplemental service providers, either for-profit or non-profit agencies. Richard (2005, December 7) suggested that when services are available, rural districts tend to use them less than urban districts.

The U.S. Department of Education is piloting an on-line tutoring service in three states through a $1.1 million grant to the Association of Educational Service Agencies out of Arlington, Virginia. Service centers in Georgia, Ohio, and Pennsylvania are participating. Participating families in rural districts receive a computer. Tutors are certified teachers who use headsets and microphones for two-hour sessions. Students can also use interactive video screens to work on problems or take tests with tutor assistance. In order for the on-line tutoring to be successful students must have technology skills, reliable technology, and be self-motivated (Richard 2005).

A Title I grant manager from Wyoming reported to *Education Week* that one of the rural schools that must offer tutoring was located on an Indian reservation that already received after-school assistance and tutoring would have to be included in those activities. Some Indian families lacked home telephone lines to allow access to on-line tutoring (Richard 2005).

The Alaska Department of Education and Early Development reported that some tutors must travel great distances by airplane to provide services in rural areas. Only about 4 percent of the eligible 14,800 Alaskan students received tutoring. Providers were scarce because few adults in villages had either the time or skills to provide tutoring and there were few on-line connections available (Richard 2005).

Outsourcing Tutoring Services

Congressional concern is rising over the NCLB Act permitting foreign companies to provide federally financed on-line tutoring to American students in low-performing schools. Companies that obtain state approval may contract with individual districts to offer tutoring services. Some of those companies provide on-line services. The U.S. Department of Education acknowledged that neither the law nor regulations for implementation addressed subcontracting or using foreign companies for tutoring (Gewertz 2005, April 20).

Education Week contacted three companies that were outsourcing tutoring services. Brainfuse, Inc., is a New York City on-line education company approved to provide supplementary services in thirty states. Brainfuse has been experimenting with overseas tutors but has not yet decided if advantages are greater than disadvantages such as the often unreliable Internet connection. Tutor.com, another New York City company, has found that using overseas tutors expanded tutoring hours given time zone differences. This company provides live homework help to students in two states. Smart Thinking, Inc., a Washington, D.C.–based company, executed a waiver assuming responsibility for overseas tutors (Gewertz 2005, April 20).

The American Federation of Teachers strongly opposes outsourcing tutoring services, stating that tutoring should be conducted by people well-versed in the curriculum and standards of the district and by someone close enough to communicate with teachers. Eight congressmen have asked the Congressional Investigative Agency to determine the extent of use of overseas tutor providers (Gewertz 2005, April 20).

India—The Overseas Tutoring Hub

Growing Stars InfoTech Limited (a subsidiary of California-based Growing Stars, Inc.) opened in 2004. This outsourced company, located in Kochi, India, offers tutoring in math, science, and English for American students in grades three through twelve. The company's growth has been phenomenal, starting with ten students and four tutors. This company now has operations in Canada, the United Kingdom, Australia, and the United States. Another six Indian companies now offer tutoring services as well. Growing Stars sets high standards for tutors who must have a master's degree in the subject they teach, as well as a teaching degree. Tutors must also have strong communication skills and attend periodic classes to polish their English accents so students can understand them (Honawar 2005, November 9).

Two areas of concern emerged when California districts required criminal background checks for service providers and the American Federation of Teachers argued that tutors should be well versed in U.S. curricula.

Also, when tutoring is on-line, there is not a clear way to determine the depth of understanding a student has obtained through the tutoring. U.S. parents have expressed satisfaction with the tutoring received through Growing Stars (Honawar 2005, November 9).

Schools Seek Tutoring Waivers

Under the NCLB Act, it has been the responsibility of the states to approve supplementary service providers for districts failing to make adequate yearly progress. Additionally, the U.S. Department of Education did not allow districts not meeting their performance goals to use federal money for their tutoring programs. Schools were required to use their own funds and to contract with outside providers for services.

Recently a policy shift was noted when Secretary Spellings allowed the Chicago district to provide tutoring with Title I funds even though it had not met its performance goals. In order to obtain this waiver for use of federal funds in their own tutoring program, Chicago schools agreed to extend the tutoring enrollment timeline and to allow a third-party evaluation of their tutoring program citywide. This waiver was not recognition of the school's progress, but a means of getting services to more eligible students (Gewertz 2005, September 7).

Similar deals appear to be in the works to enable several other large urban school districts to run their own tutoring programs even if they have failed to meet state achievement goals. A flexible agreement with the U.S. Department of Education allowed four Virginia districts to provide free tutoring to students in low-performing schools before offering students the choice of transferring to a higher-performing school. Alexandria, Newport News, Henry County, and Stafford County will be allowed to offer only tutoring during the first year that a Title I school is identified for improvement (Olson 2005, September 7). The conditions for this waiver included providing the federal government academic achievement information on students receiving tutoring, ensuring that parents have access to a variety of tutoring providers, and ensuring an increase in the number of students taking advantage of both transfer and tutoring options. The U.S. Department expressed the intent to pilot several programs across the country that switch the order of transfers and tutoring (Olson 2005).

Recently in a continuing effort to ensure free tutoring to as many students as possible, the U.S. Department of Education granted waivers to Boston and New York City. The Education Department viewed these waivers as part of a pilot project designed to boost the number of children receiving free tutoring because fewer than 20 percent of eligible children have received these services (Gewertz 2005, November 16). As many as seven other large districts could be granted waivers as part of the pilot program. There is no evidence that these school districts could not provide solid tutoring programs just because some schools are on improvement status. There was some concern expressed that districts initiating tutoring programs midyear could be placed at a disadvantage when compared with providers who have tutored a full year (Gewertz 2005, June 22).

SUMMARY AND CONCLUSIONS

As part of school reform initiations over the past decade, after-school, Saturday, and summer tutoring programs have emerged as a means of improving student achievement. Currently, tutoring programs have become the heart and soul of the NCLB Acts supplemental education services requirement. After the fourth year of implementation of the law, only about 18 percent of eligible students received tutoring during 2004–2005.

Because of the focus on parental choice, the Department of Education has supported numerous service providers to include companies that outsource tutoring services to India. There appears to be little oversight of tutoring providers to include school districts. Currently, the Department of Education is trading waivers to large urban districts to provide their own tutoring services with the use of Title I money in exchange for accepting third-party program evaluations.

Some congressmen have questioned how states should evaluate tutors' effectiveness, but there is no consensus about what constitutes success under NCLB. With the funding of supplemental services under NCLB, the demand for tutoring is greater than ever before. Most educators and parents lack the information needed to select the best provider. There is a real need to resolve the conflicts surrounding the provision of tutoring programs so that all stakeholders will know what makes a good tutor and how to measure the effectiveness of programs.

CHAPTER 4 REFLECTION QUESTIONS

1. How has Title I impacted your school and district?

2. Is there an achievement gap in your school and district?

3. If there is no gap, discuss what your school and district have done to bridge this gap and to maintain equity.

4. If there is a gap, discuss what your school and district are doing to bridge the gap and to achieve equity.

5. What tutorial programs are effective in your school and district?

6. What tutorial program ideas would you like your school and district to consider implementing?

CHAPTER 4 HELPFUL WEBSITES

Achievement Gap:
  www.learningpt.org/

Alaska Department of Education:
  www.eed.state.ak.us/

American Federation of Teachers:
  www.aft.org/

Association of Educational Service Agencies (Arlington, Va.):
  www.edlinc.org/reply-comments_5-06-02.html

Brainfuse, Inc.:
  www.brainfuse.com/index.asp

Faith-based Organizations:
  www.whitehouse.gov/government/fbci/guidance/index.html

Growing Stars, Inc.:
  www.growingstars.com/tutoringtool.htm

Minnesota Comprehensive Assessment Program:
  www.isd196.k12.mn.us/Assessment/index.cfm

Smart Thinking, Inc.:
  www.smarthinking.com/

Title I:
  www.cleweb.org/issues/title1/quality.htm

Title I—1988 Reauthorization:
  www.cleweb.org/issues/title1/quality.htm

Tutor:
  www.tutor.com/

Tutoring Programs:
  www.nwrel.org/learns/resources/startup/Startup_resources.pdf

5

Title I: Reading and Early Childhood

Man cannot discover new oceans unless he has the courage to lose sight of the shore.

—André Gide, Nobel Prize–winning author

READING FIRST

The passage of the NCLB Act has spurred renewed interest in early childhood, preschool, and kindergarten programs. The America Reads Challenge of the Clinton administration made a national commitment to the goal that every child will read independently and well by the end of the third grade. Forty percent of all U.S. children were reading below the basic level on national reading assessments (Wasik 1997). The National Assessment of Educational Progress (NAEP) showed serious deficiencies in children's ability to read, particularly in high-poverty schools. In wealthier schools, more than 20 percent of the 4th grade was unable to reach NAEP's basic reading level in 2000, while 66 percent of the 4th grade in high-poverty schools reached reading proficiency levels that year (U.S. Department of Education 2002).

Reading First is designed to assist states, districts, and schools address reading proficiency so that children can attain grade level by the end of the third grade. This program assists with implementation of reading programs and materials, assessments, and professional development that is grounded in scientifically based reading research.

Reading First Implementation

Education Week reported that more than 4,700 schools have received Reading First grants and the U.S. Department of Education expects to pump $6 billion into Reading First programs over six years. In 2000, the National Reading Panel identified five instructional factors forming the basis for Reading First programs: phonemic awareness, phonics, fluency, vocabulary, and comprehension. Pressley (2005, December 14) suggested that advocates for Reading First defended the scientific research supporting the five factors but failed to acknowledge other factors associated with reading such as variety in literature, critical understanding, motivation, writing, and discussion skills.

The narrow phonological perspective of Reading First has forced some schools to decide between the skills focus of Reading First and broader state curriculum standards. Other criticisms from schools suggest that the program is too structured, even to scripting daily lesson plans that ignore teacher knowledge and skills to decide the best approach for teaching their students (Manzo 2005, June 8).

Reading First Effectiveness

Skepticism about the effectiveness of the Reading First initiative has been building. Hard data on program effectiveness may be more than a year away, although some states provide anecdotal descriptions of benefits from Reading First. Spokespeople from the Department of Education state that the program is being implemented very well at the state and local levels.

Florida has trained about 46 percent of their K–3 teachers and reported that the percentage of students performing at grade level on the Florida state achievement test in reading increased five percentage points in Reading First schools. Texas reported Reading First provides a linking mechanism among state reading programs and initiatives. Illinois reported that coaches noted changes in teacher behavior after attending Reading First training. Reading First appears to have some impact because districts are changing their reading programs, but some may have had to change programs to comply with Reading First grant specifications (Manzo 2005, June 8).

Reading First—Criticisms and Concerns

Some states and districts reported that qualified Reading First presenters were hard to find and that the dearth of candidates to conduct required professional development workshops delayed program implementation. Some districts reported unwillingness to eliminate current reading programs to purchase the Reading First program. There appeared confusion about use of another program such as Success for All with the Reading First program. Some districts lost Reading First grants for failure to show sufficient progress on standardized tests, while other schools elected to drop the program after they determined that it did not meet their expectations (Manzo 2005, June 8).

Government Accountability Office (GAO) Investigation of Reading First

After at least three different requests to the U.S. Department of Education to scrutinize Reading First, both Republican and Democratic leaders of the U.S. Senate Education Committee have requested an investigation of this federal program. A number of specific complaints have surfaced since program implementation three years ago. Publishers and others have protested the Education Department's endorsement of specific vendors and products and prohibition of others. Success for All officials filed complaints alleging mismanagement, restriction of the organization's ability to trade, and lack of adherence to scientific information in what works in improving reading instruction. The Reading Recovery Council of North American and Cupp Publishers of Savannah, Georgia, filed similar complaints. All contend they lost clients who were told that their programs did not fit Reading First Requirements (Cavanagh, 2005, August 10).

Researchers and consultants are also alleged to have promoted products in which they had a financial stake or self-interest. Officials at the Education Department have repeatedly denied these allegations saying the responsibility is at the state level to set up unbiased procedures for selection of teaching materials, methods, and services (Manzo 2005, June 22). The publisher from Georgia alleges damages to publishers whose products were not perceived as preferred by the program because educators in all the states now know what reading programs and tests must be used to obtain Reading First grant money (Manzo 2005, October 12).

The federal investigation of Reading First will include audits of the policies and procedures involved in implementing this $1 billion per year initiative. The inquiry aims to scrutinize contracts awarded for technical assistance to states, how reviews of grant applications were conducted, and whether federal consultants followed conflict of interest procedures. The Government Accountability Office, the investigative arm of congress, is conducting a separate investigation at the request of a bipartisan group of senators (Manzo 2005, November 9).

HEAD START

Early care and education programs have done a good job in addressing social, emotional, cognitive, language, and health needs of young children, particularly those from poverty backgrounds, to prepare them for entry into kindergarten. Head Start was first initiated over forty years ago under the Lyndon Johnson administration. Currently, Head Start programs help prepare more than 900,000 disadvantaged children for kindergarten each year (Davis 2005, May 25).

A bill to reauthorize the federal Head Start preschool program was passed in May with bipartisan support, but some issues emerged as problematic. Addition of language to allow faith-based groups to hire only members of their own religion led to controversy. Only a few programs including Head Start bar faith-based groups from discriminating when they use federal money. Some believe that faith-based groups should be allowed to retain protections given them in the Civil Rights Act of 1964 (Davis 2005, May 25).

Head Start Effectiveness

Some disagreement between the Department of Health and Human Services, which has oversight of Head Start programs, and the advocacy group

National Head Start Association, emerged over a report on the effectiveness of Head Start. The study, conducted by Westat Research, followed five thousand three- and four-year-olds beginning in the fall of 2000. Children from Head Start and regular community preschool programs were compared across a variety of factors that ranged from academic readiness to health care. First-year results found that both three- and four-year-old Head Start children, when compared with children who attended regular preschool, showed small to moderate gains in pre-reading, pre-writing, and vocabulary. Neither age group showed improvements in oral comprehension, pre-math skills, or social competence. The Department of Health and Human Services interpreted the report as evidence that there was room for improvement. The advocacy group interpreted the report as proof that Head Start was having a positive impact (Davis 2005, June 15).

A Government Accountability Office (GAO) report criticized National Reporting System results as invalid and unreliable. Critics found the system inappropriate. The assistant for the Administration for Children and Families reported an analysis was being conducted to demonstrate reliability of the data and defended the system, stating that ongoing assessment of children's progress was necessary for program validation (Davis 2005, May 25).

Based on the GAO report, some congressmen expressed concern about management of Head Start and called for increased monitoring of grantees by Health and Human Services. The study by the GAO followed headline stories about some Head Start directors receiving six-figure salaries and spending money on travel and cars. Last year nearly 1,700 Head Start programs received $6.8 billion in federal funding (Davis 2005, March 23). Senate reauthorization of this large preschool program is expected after controversial issues are hammered out.

KINDERGARTEN POLICY CHANGES RECOMMENDED

Kindergarten policy varies widely from state to state. *Education Week* reported on an analysis of kindergarten statutes across the fifty states. Results show that most states do not have policy guaranteeing a full-day kindergarten. The study found no consistent state rules for funding kindergarten or to address the quality of teachers or instructional standards.

Half-day kindergartens have existed since the 1930s, but different states define *half-day* differently, with some requiring four hours and others six hours. Currently, more states are instituting full-day kindergarten programs in an effort to narrow the achievement gaps between disadvantaged and middle-class children. Some individuals indicated that kindergarten programs serve as a link between early-childhood programs and K–12 programs, so that learning standards for kindergarten programs should be connected to those for preschool and first grade. Recommendations included specifying that funding incentives for kindergarten programs should be greater than for first grade for students from disadvantaged families (Jacobson 2005, July 22).

PRE-KINDERGARTEN INITIATIVES

Background and Implications of Pre-kindergarten Programs

Early childhood programs are not new. Bracy and Stellar (2003) summarized the findings of three major preschool studies to provide evidence of program effectiveness with long-term effects. The Perry Preschool Project was a hallmark program initiated in the mid-1960s. African American children were randomly assigned to a Michigan preschool program. Educators who tested the children, interviewed parents, or taught in the program were not made aware of the random assignments in order to control for effects stemming from expectations about children. Ten categories deemed important for child development and school reading formed the framework for the program.

Both constructivist and cognitive developmental approaches were used. Studies of participants were conducted when participants reached the ages of nineteen and twenty-seven. A study at age forty is being conducted (Bracy and Stellar 2003). At age nineteen, females were found to have higher graduation rates and participants were less likely to be in special education. By age twenty-seven, Perry preschoolers had a 71 percent graduation rate or had earned a GED, in contrast to the control group who had a 54 percent graduation rate. Preschoolers earned more and were more likely to own their own homes. Members of the control group were arrested more often (Bracy and Stellar 2003).

The Abecedarian preschool has been administered by the University of North Carolina since 1972. Disadvantaged children were identified at birth. Fifty weeks of day care per year were provided until the children entered school. Adult and child language interactions were concept-based and skill-based, and social skills group orientations were included. Some children continued in the program until age eight, while others received an enriched school program.

Social work and crisis intervention were available to families of participants in the Abecedarian preschool. Children in the control group also received benefits, so that it was difficult to determine benefits of the program. As with the Perry Project, at age twenty-one females completed more years of school. Members of the Abecedarian Group were less likely to use marijuana, but no differences were found in the use of alcohol. Some effect was noted between the groups on reading and math achievement results (Bracy and Stellar 2003).

The third longitudinal study of preschool was the Chicago Child Parent Center (CPC) Program. This program did not use a control participant selection method. The program was developed by the Chicago Board of Education and adopted by twenty child centers. Extensive parent involvement was emphasized and field trips were included. By 2000, participants at age twenty-one had higher school completion rates, fewer grade retentions, and lower crime rates (Bracy and Stellar 2003).

Bracy and Stellar suggest that these three programs show evidence of preschool intervention impacting high school graduation rates and even college attendance. Quality factors for preschool programs included starting by age three, actively engaging parents, a low teacher-pupil ratio, highly qualified teachers, and a broad, intellectually rich curricula. Preschool programs are very expensive, about four to seven times more costly than regular school programs. With the passage of NCLB, preschool for disadvantaged children has been emphasized nationwide.

School Readiness Factors Identified

Jacobson (2005, February 23) reported results from a seventeen-state group consensus that identified a list of indicators of school readiness, which focus on birth through age eight and represent different phases of child development. The six broad categories selected include children, families, communities, health services, early care and education services, and schools. Emerging school readiness indicators included the number of children growing up in high poverty areas and the number having vision or hearing problems when they enter school. The report from the seventeen state groups identified a need for children entering school to have both literacy and social-emotional skills, not just one or the other (Jacobson 2005, February 23).

Concern about Developmentally Appropriate Preschool Curricula

Hatch (2002) views the proliferation of standards for early childhood education as threatening the integrity of early childhood professionals and the quality of educational experiences for young children. During the 1980s, early childhood educators resisted a movement to push curriculum expectations for primary grades downward to kindergarten and preschool programs, arguing that young children were not ready developmentally for an academic emphasis on reading and numeracy skills. According to Hatch (2002), the standards movement is a similar strategy to the push-down curriculum movement of the 1980s.

Bodrova and Leong (2005) warn educators once again about inappropriate acceleration of academic curriculum. Based upon the child development theory of Vygotsky, young children must develop fundamental cognitive, linguistic, and social-emotional competences that provide a framework for further learning. Bodrova and Leong found that children must be taught to move from reactive thinking to the ability to think before they act. Some activities are suggested to foster development of self-regulation. Scaffolding intentional play requires acting out roles in a play scenario and planning out who will play what role and what will happen. Modifying existing activities, for example, when reading, prompting children, helps them with reading comprehension and retention (Bodrova and Leong 2005).

Preschool Children Expelled More Frequently

Jacobson (2005, May 18) reported in *Education Week* that over 6 per 1,000 children are expelled from state pre-kindergarten programs compared to about 2 per 1,000 for elementary, middle, and high school programs. Expulsion rates were found to be even higher for community-managed pre-kindergarten programs. Jacobson's report is based upon information from an analysis of data from fifty-two state-financed pre-kindergarten programs in forty states.

Researchers reported that expulsion rates varied across states, but were higher in pre-kindergarten than K–12 in all states but Kentucky, Louisiana, and South Carolina. The rate of pre-kindergarten expulsions was highest in New Mexico with 21 per 1,000. Teacher responses suggested that four-year-olds were more likely to be expelled than younger children and boys were expelled at a 4.5 times greater rate than girls; African American children were twice as likely as Hispanic or white children to be expelled. Researchers suggested that pre-kindergarten teachers need more training and that if teachers had access to a mental-health professional for consultation they were less likely to expel pre-kindergarten children (Jacobson 2005, May 18).

Preschool Funding

Preschool funding issues were added to a 2001 Wyoming case, known as *Campbell County School District vs. State*, in which a coalition of low-wealth districts were required by the Wyoming Supreme Court to identify the best educational program and figure out funding. Plaintiffs argued that pre-kindergarten is now considered part of a high-quality educational experience appropriate for current times under NCLB. Plaintiffs in six other states, Colorado, Georgia, Kentucky, Nebraska, New York, and Wyoming, claim that states have the duty to cover the costs of pre-kindergarten programs for disadvantaged children (Jacobson 2005).

New Jersey is currently the only state in which the state Supreme Court ordered the legislature to pay for disadvantaged preschool children in low-income districts. If the plaintiffs are successful in Wyoming and that legislature must pay for preschool, it will be the first time that a state has had a state-financed early childhood program. Just because plaintiffs are asking for states to pay for preschool does not mean their requests will be granted. To provide a high-quality pre-kindergarten is very expensive and state funding is limited. Many states do not even have full-day kindergartens (Jacobson 2005, October 15).

The NCLB Act has focused attention upon the importance of early childhood intervention programs in the success of disadvantaged children in school programs. A number of states are developing pre-kindergarten programs and using creative means for financing them. Examples of current programs follow.

Pre-kindergarten Program Examples

Florida

Florida's voters approved a universal pre-kindergarten program in 2002. This program is expected to attract over 150,000 children. This program will be operated by private child-care and preschool providers because many schools do not have room to add classes for four-year-olds. The state is offering scholarships of $2,500 per child for this program.

Florida's Catholic Conference has raised concerns that the state scholarship is insufficient and that children from disadvantaged families would be discriminated against if additional fee-based services were required. Florida's deputy director of Early Learning stated that the pre-kindergarten law in Florida prohibits providers from excluding children from a program if their parents do not sign up for fee-based services (Jacobson 2005, April 20).

California

The Los Angeles County First Five Commission is in the process of approving the first one hundred sites that will offer the new pre-kindergarten program. This program will use tobacco tax money to pay for early childhood services. An initiative is being spearheaded to establish a universal pre-kindergarten program statewide and place this on the June 2006 ballot. This initiative would call for a pre-kindergarten program to be provided in both schools and community-based centers and integrated with child care to meet the needs of working parents (Jacobson 2005, April 20).

New Mexico

The governor has successfully pushed a pre-kindergarten bill through the legislature to provide $5 million in 2006 for a preschool program. This funding will initially be awarded to school districts, tribal governments, private preschool centers, and faith-based organizations in communities where elementary schools are not meeting state AYP goals under NCLB (Jacobson 2005, April 20).

New York City

Financing for a statewide preschool program was passed in 1997, but frozen after the September 11, 2001, attack on the World Trade Center. The level of state support lingered around $200 million, although it was supposed to reach $500 million annually over a five-year period. The New York City Board of Education allocated $6 million to open up one thousand new slots for pre-kindergarten across the city's five boroughs. The influx of children is expected to fill forty-three full-day public school classes and fourteen half-day classes.

Originally, 10 percent of the state pre-kindergarten programs were required to be housed in community-based centers, but with strong community-school cooperation, 60 percent of the pre-kindergarten children are served by community providers. Recommendations made by the Board of Regents include lowering the compulsory age for school attendance to age five instead of six and mandating full-day kindergarten. The policy recommendations also include basing financing for state pre-kindergarten programs on the regular K–12 school aid formula instead of using grants. Such policy recommendations will require legislative approval. Other policy recommendations made include (Jacobson 2005, September 21, p. 269):

- Statewide pre-kindergarten for three- and four-year-olds in all school districts.
- Stronger curriculum connections between pre-kindergarten and primary grades.
- Integrated classrooms for young children with disabilities.
- Use of the New York State University System as a resource to address academic achievement gaps through public television programs, the library, museums, and other programs.
- Improve professional development and preserve education programs.
- Greater collaboration between agencies working with children from birth to age eight.

With the implementation of the NCLB Act, many state policy makers are making expansion of early childhood services a priority. Researchers from the federally financed National Center for Early Development and Learning are examining state-financed pre-kindergarten programs to determine quality and what works and what does not (Jacobson 2005, April 20).

Pre-kindergarten Teacher Quality

Jacobson (2005, August 31) reports Florida concerns over the quality of teachers in pre-kindergarten programs. With more than ninety thousand children attending Florida pre-kindergarten programs, educators suggest that instead of just stating program goals, legislators should specify higher requirements for pre-kindergarten teachers. Currently, lead teachers must have a child development associate credential, which equals about one year of college coursework. Because Florida already lacks sufficient certified teachers, it may be more realistic to push for an associate's degree credential for teachers who would then work under the guidance of a master teacher (Jacobson 2005, August 31).

SUMMARY AND CONCLUSIONS

Early childhood education is an emerging concern nationwide. With the implementation of the NCLB Act, states are being forced to consider state pre-kindergarten and kindergarten programs for disadvantaged children so that they may enter school ready to learn. Funding issues are being considered in a number of states and plaintiff district coalitions are trying to force states to assist with funding for early childhood programs. As NCLB is reauthorized, preschool education could become part of required public education for America's children in the near future.

CHAPTER 5 REFLECTION QUESTIONS

1. What programs are in place in your school and district for early childhood?

2. What qualifications do teachers have who are teaching in these programs?

3. What changes have occurred in reading and math for early childhood since the implementation of NCLB?

4. What resources would be most helpful if your school and district chose to provide all-day early childhood programs?

5. What steps would your school and district follow to implement an all-day early childhood program?

CHAPTER 5 HELPFUL WEBSITES

Abecedarian Preschool:
www.geocities.com/heartland/forest/2468/

Administration for Children and Families:
www.acf.hhs.gov/

America Reads Challenge:
www.ed.gov/inits/americareads/index.html

Campbell County School District vs. Wyoming:
www.schoolfunding.info/states/wy/Campbell(I).pdf#search=
'Campbell%20County%20School%20vs.%20Wyoming

Chicago Public Schools:
www.cps.k12.il.us/

Chicago Child/Parent Center Program:
www.waisman.wisc.edu/cls/Program.htm

Cupp Publishers (Georgia):
www.cindycupp.com/company%20background.htm

Department of Health and Human Services:
www.hhs.gov/

Government Accountability Office:
www.gao.gov/

Head Start:
www.acf.hhs.gov/programs/hsb/

Los Angeles County First Five Commission:
www.4children.org/news/1102univ.htm

National Head Start Association:
www.nhsa.org/

National Reading Panel:
www.nationalreadingpanel.org/

New York City Department of Education:
schools.nyc.gov/default.aspx

New York State University System:
www.nysed.gov/

Perry Preschool Project:
www.highscope.org/Research/PerryProject/perrymain.htm

Reading First:
www.ed.gov/programs/readingfirst/index.html

Reading Recovery Council of North America:
www.readingrecovery.org/

Vygotsky:
en.wikipedia.org/wiki/Lev_Vygotsky

6

NCLB and School Reform: Charters and Vouchers

> If you decide to hold rigidly to your course at all costs, you may find
> that the winds rip the sails and even break off the mast. The true sailor
> . . . works with the wind.
>
> —Richard Beckhard and Reuben Harris, authors

Initiatives associated with implementation of the NCLB Act suggest that
states are carrying out an assortment of approaches to redirect the focus of
public schools. Under this four-year-old mandate, states were directed to
set aside 2 percent of their federal Title I, Part A, money for school improvement in fiscal years 2002–2003 and 4 percent in fiscal years 2004
through 2007. Ninety-five percent of these funds are expected to be allocated directly to districts with schools identified in need of improvement.
The remaining 5 percent of this money is expected to be retained at the
state level to provide a system of intensive and sustained support for
school improvement (Olson 2005, April 6).

An education consultant reported information collected from nineteen
states for *Education Week* and reported that state assistance for school improvement varied widely across states. For example, Virginia assigns high-
performing principals called turnaround specialists to low-performing
schools. Ohio uses district coaches to assist school systems with data analysis and standards-based practices. New York's 5 percent state money goes
to ten regional school support centers to work with the lowest-performing
schools.

Olson (2005, April 6) reported that the amount of school improvement money varies widely by state on a yearly basis and may have no relationship to the number of schools that are low-performing. For example, Texas identified 197 low-performing schools, but 5 percent of their Title I assistant funds should have been almost $44.4 million based on eligible children, while Virginia identified 460 schools but they were allocated only $7.8 million based on their eligible children (Olson 2005, April 6).

Federal aid was never intended to cover all the costs of school improvement. Title I funding for each state may increase or decrease annually based on the overall level of federal funding for the program and on the number of disadvantaged children in the state. Under the law, states must guarantee each district a baseline amount before financing additional school improvement so that some states may end up with less money allocated for school improvement. School reform and improvement approaches vary, with many creative programs and processes emerging with mixed results.

SCHOOL CHOICE

Under NCLB mandates, school choice is the first required sanction. If Title I schools do not meet the state adequate yearly progress (AYP) goal for two consecutive years, parents have the option to transfer their child to a nonfailing school within the same district. If all schools in the district fail to meet AYP, parents may transfer their child to a nonfailing school out-of-district. The child who transfers to a better-performing district has the option of remaining in that school until he/she completes the highest grade in that school.

The sending school district must provide transportation to the receiving school until the sending school raises its AYP level to meet state requirements. If the sending district does not have sufficient money for transportation, preference must be given to the lowest-performing children from low-income families. Schools are required to notify parents of their school improvement status in a timely manner to enable school choice decisions (Richard and Samuels 2005; U.S. Department of Education 2002; Wright, Wright, and Heath 2004).

If a Title I school fails to meet state adequate yearly progress (AYP) goals for two consecutive years, children in that school may transfer to a nonfailing school in the district under the NCLB Act. Sack (2005, March) reported that only about 1 percent of eligible students had transferred from low-performing schools. Further, districts experienced difficulty carrying out school choice provisions because schools needing improvement were not identified before the start of the school year and schools receiving transfer students were not able to maintain their class-size limits.

Limitations of School Choice

School choice has not been viewed as highly successful. Some principals of higher-rated public schools are reluctant to harm struggling schools by accepting transfer students from fellow principals' turf. Critics of school choice suggested that transfers should not be the first sanction required for underperforming schools. In the third year of not making AYP, schools are required to provide supplemental education in addition to school choice (Wright, Wright, and Heath 2004). A policy analyst for the American Association of School Administrators was quoted in *Education Week* as saying school superintendents did not promote choice because they saw little evidence of student achievement improvement based on moving students to another school in the district (Hendrie 2005, April 20).

Practical issues concerning implementing school choice also emerged. Capacity was a major problem particularly in small rural districts that do not have schools nearby for transferring. Additionally, in cities with a number of schools not making AYP, space in higher-performing schools becomes scarce. Some districts have sharply limited school transfers, sometimes openly disregarding the NCLB mandates. Some individuals suggested allowing private schools to participate in the transfer program but that was not included in the NCLB Act. In some districts, determinations of AYP cannot be made until fall because of late receipt of state test results needed to make the determination. Lack of effective parental communication about the status of their children's schools has also been problematic (Hendrie 2005).

Ideas to Remedy School Choice

Some suggestions offered for remedying school choice problems have been to offer state aid bonuses to receiving schools and to exempt the scores of transferring students from the receiving schools' accountability systems for a specified time. Currently, the law requires districts to set aside 20 percent of Title I funds for school choice and supplemental services, with a minimum of 5 percent reserved for each program (Hendrie 2005).

Others suggested that if a school does not reach AYP because of a certain subgroup, such as students with disabilities or students from racial or ethnic minorities, that subgroup should be given priority for school transfers before school choice is given to other low-performing students, and the order of sanctions should be reversed so that supplemental services are offered before school choice options. The use of data-based decision making, aligning instruction with standards, and using supplemental services have been suggested as more promising than transfers (Hendrie 2005).

The executive director of the Citizens' Commission on Civil Rights stated that district, teacher, and principal buy-in for school choice were critical to success. Fewer transfers were found in districts that did not support school choice. Currently, there is consensus that a low percentage of eligible students are participating in school choice options; whether the reason is lack of interest or lack of real choice is not known (Hendrie 2005).

SUPPLEMENTAL SERVICES

Educators appear more comfortable with supplemental services than school choice requirements under the NCLB Act. There is nothing in the way of motivation or resource incentives for implementing school choice in school districts. The number of students eligible for school transfer and supplementary services is shown in table 6.1. In general, only a few states reported more than 10 percent of their students selected the school choice option in 2003–2004. In contrast, many states saw sizable jumps in the number of students receiving tutoring (Olson 2005, March 16).

CHARTER SCHOOLS MOVEMENT

Charter schools have become one of the most visible outcomes of the school choice movement. The charter school movement has prompted innovations in the delivery of instructional services and significantly im-

Table 6.1.　2003–2004—Number of Eligible Transfer Students vs. the Percentage Who Transferred, and Number of Students Eligible for Supplemental Services vs. the Percentage Who Received Services

State	Number of Students Eligible to Transfer	Percentage of Eligible Students Who Actually Did Transfer	Number of Students Eligible to Receive Supplemental Services	Percentage of Eligible Students Who Received Supplemental Services
California	1,124,591	0.3	588,388	7.0
Connecticut	7,964	3.3	3,068	23.2
Kentucky	10,583	3.1	7,011	16.7
New York	64,872	11.4	251,248	26.7
Texas	1,925	0.0	No Data	No Data
Utah	1,980	3.1	1,294	49.1
Virginia	19,030	2.3	11,444	11.4

Source: U.S. Department of Education—NCLB States Report on Progress; Education Week Research Center (March 16, 2005, p. 21)

pacted schools by focusing upon experimentation and choice within the public education system (Harris and Lowery 2002).

Historical Background

The charter school movement began at a 1988 conference on school reform. Albert Shanker, head of the American Federation of Teachers, supported the concept of charter schools at the conference and later made a major speech concerning the charter concept at the National Press Club. The original charter concept was attributed to a report written by a former school teacher and administrator, Ray Budde (Yudof, Kirp, Levin, and Moran 2002). The original concept of charters conceived by Budde and supported by Shanker focused upon teachers, who with the support of unions and administration, could develop flexible programs within their existing schools. This concept was similar to a school-within-a-school concept.

Based upon choice-prompting efforts already in place in Minnesota, that state authorized the first charter schools in the nation in 1991. In 1992, California became the second state to embrace charter schools. One hundred charter schools were permitted but at least 10 percent of the teachers in the district, or half the teachers in any one school, were required to approve the proposed charter. California significantly liberalized charter school policy six years later when businessmen hostile to public schools gathered signatures to place a more liberal charter school initiative on the November 1998 ballot. That charter initiative allowed an unlimited number of charter schools, removed the requirement for teacher approval, and eliminated the requirement that teachers must be state certified. Currently, charter schools in California are a significant presence (Yudof et al. 2002).

Arizona's charter law passed in 1994 has the most liberal policies of any state in the nation. Arizona policy establishes multiple routes for granting charters and does not limit the total number. There is no teacher certification requirement and the regulations governing public schools are waived with the exceptions of participation in state testing, antidiscrimination requirements, and some auditing procedures. Vouchers were used for introducing completion into the Arizona education market to enable parents to obtain an education for their children at a school they deemed responsive to their needs (Yudof et al. 2002).

Major Differences between Charter and Traditional Schools

In a review of research concerning differences between charter schools and traditional schools, several major differences were identified (Finn and Kanstoroom 2002). Many charter school teachers have less experience than those in traditional schools with only about 20 percent having at least ten years' experience. Charter school pupil-teacher ratios were considerably lower than conventional schools, with the number of students per class ranging around fifteen. Charter schools were much more likely than traditional schools to employ noncertified teachers.

Personnel issues differ. Many charter schools only offer one-year contracts and about 80 percent had terminated a teacher at the end of the year or even at midyear for low performance. Charter schools were found to have much higher teacher attrition rates than conventional schools. Some charter schools paid higher salaries for hard-to-fill teaching areas. Merit pay for performance was utilized in about 50 percent of the charters examined. Many disregarded advanced degrees and experience in hiring teachers. Many charters used a business model and based pay strictly on performance. Finn and Kanstoroom (2002) suggested that charter school administrators did things differently in the area of personnel issues when they were not tied to bureaucratic restraints imposed by states on public schools.

Charter School Authorization

Charters are contracts between two parties, the school operator and the authorizer (Palmer and Gau 2005). For charter schools to be successful, both parties must do their jobs. The school operator must meet contract obligations to run an effective school that delivers the promised outcomes. The major role of the authorizer is to provide assistance, oversight, and to renew a contract for successful performance.

Charter schools were first initiated in the early 1990s in Minnesota. Palmer and Gau's (2005) research found that charter authorizers had monitored charters and that 138 revocations of contracts had occurred across twenty-four states. Conversely, these researchers reported that, based on their data, many authorizers were not balancing accountability and flexibility very well. A major finding of this study showed that the perception across twenty-four states was charter schools were not well accepted by local school districts and they were not well understood by the public. Concerns were expressed over insufficient internal and external accountability for authorizers because authorizers were not required to report to a state institution and they did not conduct self-evaluations of their practices.

Local school boards were found not to be good authorizers although they authorized 93 percent of the charter schools in the study. Local boards are often influenced by local politics or charter adverse education interest groups. Of significance, local boards do not have adequate infrastructure to support authorizing charter contracts.

States serving more charter schools with fewer authorizers were perceived as having more effective practices. The Palmer and Gau (2005) study reported a total of 502 different entities were acting as authorizers across twenty-four states, which included special state charter boards, university or community college boards, city mayor's offices, nonprofit organizations, regional or intermediate school district boards, and (the majority of authorizers) local school district boards. Illinois and Texas were exceptions that local boards did not make good authorizers. In Houston and Chicago, local boards authorized so many charters that they assigned one or more staff exclusively to authorizing tasks. In Wisconsin, local boards authorize charters but these charters focus primarily upon services for at-risk students and represent little competition from public schools (Palmer and Gau 2005).

State boards of education were found to have difficulty as authorizers of charter schools particularly in states where board members are elected. Additionally, state boards usually depend upon the staff of the state's board of education to conduct authorizer duties and state departments may not have the infrastructure to support this role. Palmer and Gau (2005) found two major factors for effective authorizers of charter schools: the ability to make data-driven decisions not political decisions, and having enough staff dedicated to the tasks of authorizing who are not bound by traditional compliance-based accountability systems. They concluded that the operation of successful charter schools depended upon the successful work of those who authorize them.

Constitutionality of Charter Schools Questioned

On November 29, 2005, the Ohio Supreme Court heard arguments concerning the constitutionality of the state's system of charter schools in *Ohio Congress of Parents and Teachers vs. State of Ohio Board of Education* (Robelen 2005, December 7). The concept of charter schools is not popular with public school groups, although Ohio has nearly 300 charter schools, more than most other states. The plaintiffs want a decision that makes charter schools and their current funding unconstitutional, to force lawmakers to either change the state law or halt the funding to charter schools by the fall semester of 2006. Governance of charters appears to be a major issue.

The plaintiffs argued that a school is not a public school if it is managed by a for-profit corporation. Ohio has 80 public charter schools that do not discriminate; they hire state-certified teachers; they are publicly funded; they do not charge tuition; there are no entrance examinations; and they are nonsectarian. The major issue the plaintiffs expressed was that local school boards should have control of public charter school governance. The senior solicitor in the Ohio Attorney General's Office argued that local control by school districts is not required because charters are funded solely by the state. The defense stated that charters face stronger accountability measures than public schools because if parents and students do not like them, they leave along with their funding. So far, the state has not done an appropriate job holding charter schools accountable for student performance and achievement has been lackluster (Robelen 2005).

Emerging Charter Schools

Hawaii

While the Hawaii Department of Education is unable to provide additional money for the state's charter schools, the Office of Hawaiian Affairs (OHA) has allocated $2.2 million to fourteen charter schools that focus on the needs of native Hawaiians. Four of the fourteen charter schools are Hawaiian language immersion schools; two offer bilingual instruction in Hawaiian and English, while the other eight schools offer Hawaiian language classes. The fourteen charter schools serve about 1,700 students.

Hawaii has twenty-seven New Century Charter Schools created to provide a variety of innovative education techniques, but these schools receive less operative aid and no money for facilities in exchange for greater autonomy from the state. Hawaiian charter schools are supposed to receive $6,500 per student, but there was not enough money to cover about 800 of the 5,500 charter school students this year. During 2003–2004, charter school students were reported to outperform students attending traditional Hawaiian schools on state achievement tests (Jacobson 2005, October 26).

New Orleans

After Hurricane Katrina, the New Orleans district school board decided to reopen its first buildings not as public schools but as charter schools. The Algiers neighborhood on the city's West bank converted all thirteen schools there to charter status. Many individuals viewed the charter vote as a first step toward enlarging the state's role in the district. The charter application shows the availability of a $20.9 million grant from the U.S. Department of Education to repair and expand public charter schools in Louisiana (Gewertz 2005, October 19).

The charter application was developed without the input of the acting superintendent and the governor signed an executive order waiving key portions of the state's charter school law such as the requirement that conversion of a school to charter status had to be approved by the school's faculty and parents. Many individuals expressed concern at the lack of public input and perceived the change as a state takeover. The state role in New Orleans is unclear, but the state superintendent noted, "We're not going to rebuild a failing system, we want to rebuild a school system that *works*" (Gewertz 2005, October 19, p. 15).

State Charter Policy Changes

Texas

The charter law was first adopted in 1995 and revised in 1997 and 2001 to require compliance with new requirements. Texas has more than 80,000 students in 313 charter schools trailing only those of California in enrollment. Texas has some very outstanding charter schools such as the fast-growing chain of schools using the Knowledge Is Power Program (KIPP) which started in Houston. KIPP is now based in San Francisco and has a network of 38 schools in 15 states and the District of Columbia. KIPP has been widely praised for attaining academic results with disadvantaged children (Hendrie 2005, February 16).

In general, Texas charter schools have lagged well behind their district-run counterparts on state achievement tests, but studies suggest that charter school students make gains at a faster rate (Hendrie 2005). Based on a report by the Progressive Policy Institute, Texas needs to overhaul its charter school policies so that the poorest ones do not drag down the state's entire charter sector. Changes suggested by this report include making it easier to close down failing schools, paperwork reduction, granting exemptions to the state's charter cap for high-performing charters, and slashing the number of charter schools that are considered alternative charters outside the regular school accountability system (Hendrie 2005).

The teacher affiliate of the American Federation of Teachers opposes lifting the charter cap because too many charter schools are not being held to the same standards of academic and fiscal accountability as public schools. The Texas Education Agency and the State Commissioner of Education are in the process of making regulatory changes to address some of the shortcomings cited in the Institute Report (Hendrie 2005).

Ohio

Ohio has recently amended the state's charter school law. The new law caps the number of new charter schools that can open over the next two years to sixty. Half must be sponsored by school districts and half by education-oriented, nonprofit organizations and Ohio's public colleges and universities. Charter school operators that met performance standards may be granted waivers to open more schools.

A 2003 law capped the total number of charter schools at 250 and withdrew the state board of education's power to grant charters. Ohio now has 249 publicly financed charters serving 62,000 students. Under the new law, the maximum number of schools a charter school sponsor can authorize is fifty. Charter schools now face sanctions and they will be closed if they fail to make AYP for three consecutive years.

Concerns about the Charter Movement

The Arizona charter law exempts charter schools from state statutes and public school rules of governor's boards and school districts. Charter schools must comply with federal and state mandates that involve health, safety, and civil rights. The blanket waiver relieves much of the bureaucratic pressure faced by public schools (Garn 1998).

Concern has been expressed at the total lack of oversight provided charter schools by the State Board of Education, the State Board for Charter Schools, and the Arizona Department of Education. Charter schools were required to complete an annual written report demonstrating progress toward written charter objectives, but there was no formal evaluation of this self-report. Twenty-two charter schools were granted a waiver from following either the Uniform System of Financial Records or the charter school version. The twenty-two schools need only follow generally accepted accounting principles (Garn 1998).

Arizona policy makers have taken explicit steps to ensure a competitive market approach by making parents the primary accountability mechanism. For instance, if a charter school meets parent expectations, parents keep children enrolled. Conversely, if parents are not happy they will remove their child and the school will be forced to close because of low enrollment. Garn (1998) suggests that the Arizona charter school policy devalued teacher professionalism because teachers are not protected by tenure provisions and can be hired and fired with minimal due process. Teachers are not required to have certification.

Massachusetts for-profit charter schools have been accused of ignoring the needs of students with disabilities. Zollers and Ramanthan (1998) accuse two Edison charter schools of returning students with disabilities to local school districts. Special education directors in districts with for-profit charters reported that charter school personnel informed parents of students with disabilities that their child would be better served in the public schools. Charter school operators complained that their small size and lack of funds made it difficult to serve students with disabilities.

The UCLA Charter School Study reported in the *Kappan* (Wells and Research Associates 1998) suggests that California charters may not support the basic premises upon which charter reforms were founded. Wells and Associates studied seventeen different charter schools in ten California districts. Findings suggest that student achievement data for accountability purposes was not consistent and that 14 percent of the charter schools did not use standardized tests or collect baseline data. Charter school success was found to be highly dependent on a visionary, well-connected leader who was able to draw together diverse local community members, parents, and teachers, and network inside the school community.

In contrast to the assumption that charter schools provide greater access to disadvantaged groups having few choices, Wells and Associates (1998) found charter schools provided only some families increased educational choices because charter schools have greater latitude in choosing which parents and students they will accept. Charter schools have more power than public schools in shaping their educational communities. This situation was interpreted by public schools as an unfair advantage so that public schools did not change their behavior because of competition, as was visualized by supporters of the charter movement. Relationships between charter and public schools were found to be nonexistent, benign, or poor (Wells and Research Associates 1998).

To date, charter schools have escaped serious judicial challenge. A permissive legal environment has not led to consensus among educators about the implications of charter schools. Some believe these schools can improve educational achievement, enhance parental involvement, stimulate teacher innovation, and promote accountability. Others remain doubtful that charters are a solution for the public school system's problems. However, political support for school choice has mushroomed over the past decade and the charter school movement has had significant impact.

VOUCHERS

An educational voucher is a public grant that provides parents with funds to send their children to public or private schools of their choice. Thirteen years ago, President George H. W. Bush proposed giving $1,000 in federal scholarships to middle- and low-income students, which parents could use at any accredited school. This was called "The G.I. Bill for Kids" (Alexander 2002, p. 699). This was not a transfer of money from public to nonpublic schools but was proposed as a means to equalize school spending per pupil nationwide. The NCLB Act requires states to give options to students in persistently low-rated schools. Greater choice is made possible by providing families with money in the form of a voucher that can be used for tuition in any participating school, usually including both public and private schools (Metcalf and Tait 1999).

Historical Background

The idea of school choice in the form of vouchers originated in the mid-1950s with economist Milton Friedman, a professor at the University of Chicago. Friedman argued that vouchers would improve educational efficiency by placing schools in a competitive, free-market position (Miller 1999). Friedman (1962) saw a universal voucher system as a way to allow government to continue financing public education while separating it from its administration and establishing a true free market arena in which choice would be equal for all. Competition would be fierce and only the best schools would survive.

Other advocates suggest that through vouchers public schools will become market-driven and become more efficient, run more like a business, will more effectively fulfill their mission, will become more accountable to their customers, the public, and they will either improve or close. This economic rationale for education vouchers is a hypothesis that to date has little objective supporting data (Ramirez 1998).

Throughout the 1960s, school vouchers were not seriously considered. During the 1970s, some individuals advocated use of school vouchers as a means of empowering parents and equalizing educational opportunity because poor families have little or no choice in where they reside; they often live in poor neighborhoods near dangerous and ineffective schools (Fowler 2004; Metcalf and Tait 1999). In 1980, Ronald Reagan advocated both tuition tax credits and vouchers in speeches, but legislation support- ing school vouchers was defeated (Fowler 2004).

Legislation favoring vouchers has had a rocky history. Mendez (1999) noted that this issue was brought before the public twenty-two times since 1966 and rejected by voters twenty-one times. In voucher elections, American voters have rejected tax support for private and religious schools. Opponents voice concern about vouchers' lack of effectiveness, the damage done to public schools, and the racial, ethnic, and economic segregation vouchers will cause. Advocates cite improvements that will accrue to education through increased competition, greater family in- volvement, and increased effectiveness and accountability they believe vouchers can create (Miner 1998).

Currently vouchers leading to school choice have moved into govern- ment policy. Vouchers can be considered redistributive policy that shifts resources in the form of money or power within the educational estab- lishment. Vouchers reallocate the districts' power to assign students and state funds to schools and give this power to parents through school choice options (Fowler 2004).

Examples of Voucher Programs

The No Child Left Behind Act has helped fuel school choice through vouchers. The Milwaukee parental choice program was initiated in 1990. This program provided up to $2,500 in the form of vouchers for private school tuition. The funds for the vouchers were deducted from state gen- eral equalization aid to the Milwaukee Public Schools. Initially, this pro- gram provided vouchers to 341 low-income students to enroll in seven private schools. Three program evaluations have been conducted. The fundamental effectiveness was judged by comparing data from partici- pants and families with data from nonparticipating students and families. Data included test scores, parent and student survey data, and school records. Voucher families cited educational quality as the most important factor in their decision to participate in school choice.

Other highly rated reasons cited included teaching style and approach, disciplinary environment, and general atmosphere of the school. Student achievement in the fourth year of the voucher program after controlling for prior achievement and demographic variables of income and family size was not significantly different for voucher students and low-income public school students remaining in their home schools (Metcalf and Tait 1999; Witte 1999). Witte wonders if anyone believes that middle and up-per-middle income private school families will remain content to continue to pay tuition when everyone else is receiving other free public education or vouchers.

In June 1999, the governor of Florida signed the Opportunity Scholar-ship Program, a sweeping revision of the Florida education code that could qualify students for vouchers. The value of a voucher equals the per-student funding allocated to the student's district. The day after the voucher plan became effective, a lawsuit was filed by the Florida chapter of the American Civil Liberties Union (ACLU) challenging the constitu-tionality of the voucher program (Elam 1999).

Constitutionality of Vouchers

The central federal question concerns whether the participation of sectar-ian schools violates the First Amendment's Establishment Clause which prohibits governmental action that advances religion. Florida's Opportu-nity Scholarship Program violated the Florida Constitution on three counts (Elam 1999, p. 84). Article 1, paragraph 3, states "No revenue of the state or any political subdivision or agency thereof shall ever be taken from the public treasury directly or indirectly in the aid of any church, sect, or religious denomination or in aid of any sectarian institution." Ar-ticle IX, paragraph 1, requires the state to provide "A uniform, efficient, safe, secure, and high-quality system of free public schools." Article IX, paragraph 6, provides that "The income derived from the state school fund shall, and the principal of the fund may be appropriated, but only to the support and maintenance of free public schools."

The First Amendment constitutes a separation between church and state that is a significant democratic tradition. Recently the United States

Supreme Court has been relaxing its interpretations of the Establishment Clause and appears more willing to allow state money to flow to sectarian schools than in the past.

For example, *Agostini vs. Felton* (1997) found no violation of the Establishment Clause in providing Title I compensatory education for parochial schools. According to the majority of the courts funds were paid directly to the student, not the school (Elam 1999).

In the *Zelman vs. Simmons-Harris* (2002) decision, the Supreme Court upheld the constitutionality of a voucher program in Cleveland, Ohio. The Cleveland program was established as a program to provide educational choices for students of a persistently failing school district in Cleveland that had high dropout rates and low student achievement. In this case, the program was determined to be one of true private choice and neutral with respect to religion. Additionally, the program provided direct assistance to a large class of individuals without reference to religion and allowed the participation of all district schools, religious and nonreligious (Belfield and Levin 2002).

The No Child Left Behind Act of 2001 emphasizes school choice. Most of the school choice agenda will involve public school programs. However, if a school continues to be low-performing after three consecutive years, the students are eligible for supplemental education services from public or private providers and these can include both tutoring and private school tuition (Belfield and Levin 2002).

Examples of Current Voucher Legislation

In Ohio, the governor is proposing the expansion of the state's eight-year-old $17.9 million voucher program currently operating in Cleveland. The proposed 2006 budget would fund $9 million for new scholarships. This program proposes $3,500 per student from elementary and middle schools in which two-thirds of the students failed both math and reading tests for three consecutive years. If approved, some 2,600 students could be eligible for vouchers. The Ohio School Boards Association adamantly opposes this proposition (Richard and Samuels 2005).

In Texas, the governor has proposed a pilot voucher program for students in low-rated schools in some of the state's largest districts (Richard and Samuels 2005). Florida's commissioner of education suggests that vouchers are the most effective incentive the state can provide for its lowest-performing students. Since the Opportunity Scholarships began in 1999, twenty-one public schools have received low-performing status. About seventy-two students have used scholarship funds to attend the Archbishop Curley–Notre Dame High School in Miami's Little Haiti section. Because the $4,355 Opportunity Scholarships do not cover the school's $7,000 annual tuition, the private high school has had to raise additional money for the students to attend.

A spokesperson for the Miami, Florida, school stated that the vouchers were not being used to support religion, but to support parents. The individual who managed the scholarships for the 272,003-student Broward County schools stated that the program may work for some families, but it presents problems for others. About 1,900 Broward County students use the vouchers. Parents have not been able to determine the quality of the private schools participating in the program (Manzo 2005, May 25).

Recent Voucher Policy

In August 2005, Hurricane Katrina struck the southern coast, severely disabling schools in Louisiana, Mississippi, and Alabama. In September 2005, Hurricane Rita struck Louisiana and Texas. The Department of Education has estimated that 372,000 children and their families have been displaced, many of them still unable to return to their homes and schools. In four of the hardest hit parishes in Louisiana, 32 percent of the 187,000 children attending K–12 schools were enrolled in private schools. According to Holland (2005) the national average for students in grades K–12 enrolled in private schools is 11 percent. Many displaced families have moved to surrounding states, increasing the burden on already overloaded school districts. A number of displaced families have enrolled their children in private or secular schools.

Financing Displaced Students

Various solutions to compensate schools that have taken in displaced students have been proposed. In mid-September, two Louisiana senators introduced a bill to provide educational aid to schools serving Louisiana's displaced school children. The bill provided for grants to public, private, or religious schools in the amount of $4,000 for each student (Alliance for School Choice 2005, September 22). On October 27, 2005, a House committee rejected a proposal that would have reimbursed all schools that have taken in displaced students. The bill was defeated 26–21 because committee members deemed the program was an attempt to create a religious-schools voucher system (Fagan 2005).

President George W. Bush proposed about $2 billion in education relief that could be used in public, private, or religious schools. His plan reserved up to $488 million to assist in the payment of private school tuition. This one-year program would provide up to $7,500 of a family's per-child tuition costs at a secular or religious school (Fagan 2005). Voucher opponents and education groups opposed the proposal.

On November 4, 2005, the Senate approved a plan to aid school districts hit by Hurricane Katrina and those districts who took in displaced students. The $1.66 billion relief bill appropriates $450 million for districts damaged by the storm and $1.2 billion to help public, private, and religious schools with displaced students. Schools would receive $6,000 per student or $7,500 per student with a documented disability (Davis 2005, November 4).

SUMMARY AND CONCLUSIONS

A common feature of school choice programs is that they are designed to increase the range of opportunities for education available to all students; yet, at the same time, they often present conflicting support in the public and private arena. Charter schools have emerged as a major choice option for parents. Results of charter school impact on student achievement are mixed. Some believe charter schools can improve educational achievement, enhance parental involvement, stimulate teacher innovation, and promote accountability. Others remain doubtful that charters are a solution for the public school's problems. Charter schools remain a major choice component under NCLB.

Vouchers are based on free market concepts associated with economist Milton Friedman. Some believed that through vouchers, schools would become market-driven and run more efficiently like businesses, and become more accountable to parents as customers. Vouchers were believed to make schools more accountable to either improve or close, based on a competitive market. The use of vouchers to date shows little evidence to support the free-market theory.

Currently, vouchers leading to school choice have shifted into a redistributive policy that changes resources or power within the education realm. In 1997, the Supreme Court case *Agostini vs. Felton* (1997) found no violation of the constitution's establishment clause in providing Title I compensatory education for parochial schools because these schools were determined to be private choice and neutral with respect toward religion. There are two main issues concerning vouchers—the separation of church and state and use of federal funds to give parents school choice through vouchers. Policy makers will need to view the complex issue of vouchers with caution since this strategy has the potential to alter the role of public education toward privatization and a market economy.

The issue of school vouchers is not simple. While vouchers could solve the school choice problem for some parents whose children attend low-performing schools, it would open the door to funding all schools. This debate will continue as states try to find a solution to school improvement while ensuring all children equal access to a high-quality education. Policy makers will need to proceed cautiously, since the school privatization movement has the potential to alter the nature and role of public education in the United States.

CHAPTER 6 REFLECTION QUESTIONS

1. What is the status of charter schools in your district?

2. Talk with a charter school administrator and identify differences in these programs as compared to your school.

3. How do parents consider charter schools in your area?

4. What is the perception among educators in your district/school regarding charter schools?

5. What is your understanding of vouchers and the role they play in school choice?

6. In what ways might vouchers strengthen the traditional public school?

7. In what ways might vouchers threaten the traditional public school?

CHAPTER 6 HELPFUL WEBSITES

American Association of School Administrators:
  www.aasa.org/

Archbishop Curley–Notre Dame High School:
  www.acnd.net/

Charter Schools:
  www.essentialschools.org/

Citizens' Commission on Civil Rights:
  www.cccr.org/

Edison Schools:
  www.edisonschools.com/

Educational Vouchers:
  www.edreform.com/index.cfm?fuseAction=section&pSectionID=
    14&cSectionID=37

First Amendment Establishment Clause:
  www.law.cornell.edu/wex/index.php/First_amendment

G.I. Bill of Rights for Kids:
  www.pbs.org/now/society/edhistory.html

Hawaii Department of Education:
  doe.k12.hi.us/

Hawaiian Language Immersion Schools:
  www.angelfire.com/hi2/hawaiiansovereignty/hawlangimmersion
    histpurpose.html

Knowledge Is Power Program:
  www.kipp.org/

Massachusetts For-profit Charter Schools:
  www.npr.org/templates/story/story.php?storyId=1001524

Milton Friedman:
  www.hoover.org/bios/friedman.html

CHAPTER 6 HELPFUL WEBSITES (*continued*)

Milwaukee Public Schools:
   mpsportal.milwaukee.k12.wi.us/portal/server.pt

New Century Charter Schools:
   www.newcenturycharter.com/

Ohio Congress of Parents/Teachers vs. State Board of Education:
   www.eagleforum.org/psr/2004/aug04/psraug04.html

Ohio School Boards Association:
   www.osba-ohio.org/

Opportunity Scholarship Program:
   www.floridaschoolchoice.org/Information/OSP/

Ray Budde:
   www.boston.com/news/globe/obituaries/articles/2005/06/21/ray_
      budde_coined_phrase_charter_schools/

School Choice:
   www.schoolchoiceinfo.org/

State Board of Charter Schools:
   www.asbcs.state.az.us/asbcs/

UCLA Charter School Study:
   www.edreform.com/index.cfm?fuseAction=pressRelease&news
      Year=1998&pSectionID=&cSectionID=55

Uniform System of Financial Records:
   www.azleg.state.az.us/ars/15/00271.htm

Zelman vs. Simmons-Harris:
   www.ed.gov/news/pressreleases/2002/06/06272002c.html

7

Restructuring

Managing change in complex organizations is like steering a sailboat
in turbulent water and stormy winds.

—Richard Beckhard and Reuben Harris, authors

COMPREHENSIVE SCHOOL REFORM

Odden (2000) defined comprehensive school reform as implementing and
sustaining schoolwide change through a complete restructuring endeavor.
Comprehensive school reform is a growing phenomenon particularly with
the implementation of the NCLB Act in 2001. Comprehensive school reform began in the early 1990s with some whole-school designs such as Accelerated Schools and Success for All. Some comprehensive designs adopt
high standards, but include instructional strategies that provide assistance
for students who are functioning below grade level. Such models address
difference groupings for students and different schedules. Block scheduling resulted from such efforts. Other strategies cover planning time for
teachers, home outreach strategies, use of computer-assisted technology,
and professional development. Implementing a comprehensive reform
model represents a major educational change effort (Odden 2000).

According to Odden (2000), the costs of different restructuring designs
varied. For example, many designs did not address class size. Training
costs varied from $22,000 to $75,000 and some designs did not include
technology, while others required considerable technology and some

ignored strategies for at-risk students. He concluded that good cost estimates are needed, as well as good estimates of the impact of comprehensive school reform models on student achievement.

PROFESSIONAL LEARNING COMMUNITIES

The idea of improving schools by developing professional learning communities is now popular and the term has been used to describe group collaboration for educational benefit. For example, a grade-level teaching
team, a high school department, an entire school or district, or the state
Department of Education have been described as professional learning
communities.

DuFour (2004) identified major concepts associated with the term *professional learning community*. First, school mission statements have
shifted from ensuring that students are taught to ensuring that students
learn. The efforts of a professional learning community must become
more collaborative to ensure student learning. Efforts focusing on timely
identification of student needs must become based on interventions rather
than remediation and directives requiring students to seek additional help
and extra time to succeed.

Second, educators must build a collaborative structure. Collaboration
must move beyond teachers' consensus on operational procedures such as
consistency with tardiness to ensure teachers work in teams to analyze
data and plan instruction. DuFour (2004) suggests development of common formative assessments and authentic assessments. He states that
schools must devote time and energy to the implemented curriculum
rather that the intended curriculum and closely examine the attained curriculum. DuFour (2004) suggests that building a professional learning
community is a matter of will because professionals who are truly collaborative will find a way to work together.

DuFour's third concept refers to professional learning communities
judging their own effectiveness on student results. Teachers can work in
isolation and analyze their data, but when teacher teams collaborate each
teacher then has access to new ideas, strategies, and materials from the entire team for use in improvement.

A true professional learning community model can be a powerful new
way of working together that impacts the practices of the school, but ini-

tiating and sustaining such a model requires continued hard work. The rise or fall of a professional learning community does not depend on the merits of the concept, but on the commitment and persistence of the educators themselves (DuFour 2004).

SCHOOL LEARNING COMMUNITIES

While professional learning communities emphasize collaboration and teamwork among school personnel, school learning communities include educators as well as students, parents, and community partners who work together to enhance student learning opportunities (Epstein and Salinas 2004). School community partnerships begin with the school improvement team. Community involvement plans are included in the school improvement goals and promising practices have been identified through the National Network of Partnership Schools.

Epstein and Salinas (2004) identified multiple ways of encouraging community involvement. A major focus was upon communication, collaboration, and shared decision making. Some examples provided discussed an early childhood center in Buffalo, New York, that conducted a diversity celebration program that included more than eight different cultural groups in their learning community. An Illinois junior high school held evening discussions about adolescence to assist parents to share effective strategies and network with each other. They also held a weekly activity for sending information home, created a database for volunteers, conducted family literacy nights, and celebrated Dad's day. These activities were limited to goals in the school improvement plan.

Most schools conduct activities to involve parents, but they rarely have a well-developed, goal-linked program they can sustain year to year. With NCLB requirements for parent involvement, schools are now encouraged to develop active effective school learning communities.

SCHOOL REDESIGN

Evans (2003) describes difficulties found in implementing a restructuring project in a large high school in Massachusetts. Difficulties were encountered with various components such as students, parents, faculty, and the central office. The principal of this large urban high school worked through the facts of reform to break the school into five small schools of four hundred students. This school had two thousand students, a large achievement gap, clashes of philosophy between faculty, and a general lack of accountability.

Evans (2003) found that 60 percent of the student body were students of color and were not used to high expectations for everyone. Although these students touted diversity, they remained with their own group. Restructuring rocked everyone. Students at the high end of the spectrum complained about low expectations and bad behavior of other students now with them who did not do their homework. Evans (2003) found that shifting a culture from one with high demands for selected groups while tolerating mediocre work from another group to a community that had high expectations for all created major problems.

Implementing restructuring with faculty was also difficult. Nearly 20 percent of the faculty had been at the school at least thirty years. They found students hard to teach and blamed students for their lack of achievement. Many teachers lacked motivation for collaboration or for viewing their students' work with colleagues and discussing it. Faculty had many legitimate concerns such as how to teach mixed groups of students or how to teach students who had experienced nothing but failure for years. The faculty expressed many concerns, such as what to do with students with disabilities, lack of sufficient time for teachers, no faculty credentials for counseling but they were expected to counsel students, and so on (Evans 2003).

White parents opposed restructuring and organized against the change. The goals of knowing all students well in a smaller school situation and having high standards for all did not make sense to some parents. Evans (2003) emphasized five themes in communication with parents: challenges for students, student connection with an advisor, the small school concept would provide a sense of community for students, the schools would be fair because of equal size and resource allocations, and teachers would have their own learning community in the smaller schools with more time to plan and prepare for teaching.

The principal left this school after the second year of the restructuring effort, citing lack of central office support for full hiring authority. When curriculum coordinators were allowed to hire teachers and they cut some deals, Evans felt the restructuring effort was doomed to failure. Major tasks identified for this restructuring effort focused on the school culture, student needs, capacity and talent of faculty, development of a plan for change, and modifying it as implementation occurred. This case study emphasized pitfalls that can happen during implementation even with initial support and considerable planning.

RESTRUCTURING AS A RESULT OF LOW SCHOOL PERFORMANCE

High stakes testing can have negative outcomes for schools. Testing required by NCLB takes the form of public reporting of test results, the prevention of student promotions and high school graduation, and possibly school takeovers if that school continues to exhibit low student performance. Currently, the quality of a school is judged almost entirely upon how well students perform on state tests. Vogler and Kennedy Jr. (2003) describe the restructure of the curriculum in a Lawrence, Massachusetts, school to raise test scores. Two new test preparation programs were added to the curriculum in all Lawrence schools, Literacy Enhancement Test Sophistication (LETS) and Numeracy Enhancement Test Sophistication (NETS). These programs contained fifteen weeks of scripted lessons for grades 3, 4, 6, 7, 8, and 10. In order to implement the test preparation programs, reading was eliminated for the fifteen weeks and the other core courses shortened to about forty-three minutes per day. This school system felt there was no alternative but to restructure the curriculum to accommodate test preparation because of low student test results.

SCHOOL TAKEOVERS

Philadelphia School District Takeover

In 2001, the Commonwealth of Pennsylvania initiated a takeover of the academically and financially distressed Philadelphia Systems, the seventh-largest system in the United States. This system served 200,000 students in 250 schools. Multiple private sector organizations were given responsibility for school operations. Edison Schools were responsible for 20 schools. Philadelphia's students made significant achievement gains and exceeded the gain of all but one of the 50 largest school systems for the 2003 school year (Whittle 2005).

The chief executive officer of Philadelphia did several things to ensure that the public, private, multi-provider model was successful. A standardized curriculum and instruction based on best practices was used to drive achievement. Online lesson plans, district progress monitoring, and support materials were provided to teachers. The Philadelphia takeover plan required dramatic academic reform, mandated accountability and competition, and increased resources to achieve goals (Whittle 2005).

The School Reform Commission arranged for companies as well as universities and community organizations to each manage 20 percent of the district's schools. The University of Pennsylvania and Temple University were involved. As a result, companies, nonprofits, and regular district schools competed to produce the best possible results. Private-sector organizations, companies, and universities might be uniquely suited to addressing unique achievement needs such as development of sophisticated benchmarking assessment systems or intensive cost-efficient professional development programs (Whittle 2005).

Texas School District Takeover

In May 2005, the state commissioner of education replaced the seven-member elected school board of the Wilmer-Hutchins Independent School District with five appointees and replaced the district's interim superintendent with an administrator from a neighboring school system. The state had periodically placed monitors and management teams in this district over the past twenty years. Such steps led to temporary relief, but never produced a sustained management turnover of this district.

A number of issues surfaced concerning this district to include documentation of cheating on state mandated achievement tests. The district had a projected budget deficit of $5.7 million. The appointed board must decide whether to close the school district and send its students to a nearby district. Some feel it would be in the best interests of the students to split up the district. Many Wilmer-Hutchins students live in Dallas and its inner suburbs. The district also borders Lancaster and Ferris I.S.D. (Hoff 2005, May 18).

Mayoral Takeovers

The balance of control in educational decisions has never been one of logical analysis, but has evolved as part of a series of political bargains and perceptions about the capacity of alternative institutions. In recent years, individuals outside traditional educational governance have exhibited interest in participating in educational policy making. One means of initiating significant change in educational systems is to circumvent the existing decision makers by changing the governance structure itself. Under the progressive model of the early 1900s bureaucratic routines became a way to protect a superintendent's authority and to deal with inadequate resources at the expense of innovation and productivity.

Reformers of the 1990s contended that it would take mayors to restore central accountability and serve as a link to voter preferences. Mayors can no longer avoid school-related issues politically because of the growing belief that schools are a critical factor in economic development and schools generate considerable tax dollars, which some mayors would like to control. The mayors of Chicago, Boston, and Cleveland have received considerable support at both city and state levels for their efforts to assert control over education.

Political integration with mayors as leaders is based on the belief that policy becomes more effective with clear and direct lines of accountability from elected officials to the public that elected them. There is a current belief in a new breed of mayors who can improve education and avoid past mistakes. These new mayors have formed an informal network and symbolize a radical break from their predecessors. They speak the language of public management and are not afraid to confront strong political interests including teacher unions, civil rights leaders, and the Christian Coalition (Kirst and Bulkley 2004).

Opponents of mayoral control of education suggest that a school board appointed by the mayor would result in less democracy and that mayoral controlled contracts could result in machine politics where contracts are traded for campaign contributions. More efforts at mayoral takeovers seem likely. A key issue is whether mayoral control can improve student achievement. Reformers will continue to use governance and organizational changes to improve education even though such mechanisms have not offered proven practices for improving classroom instruction (Kirst and Bulkley 2004).

SCHOOLS IN MALLS

Since 1998, the Simon Property Group, the United States' largest mall developer, has partnered with local public school systems to open nineteen alternative public schools located in shopping malls in eleven states. Lafayette Square's school in Indianapolis is the newest and largest, with a two-hundred-student capacity. Mall schools maintain a fifteen-to-one student-teacher ratio and require students to sign a behavioral contract and learn job skills.

Molnar (2005) suggests that as Simon Property Group moves the schoolhouse into a shopping center, marketers burrow into public education. This trend is making public schools less like education institutions and more like shopping malls, where students spend their free time. The reasons schools are willing to partner with businesses like the Simon Group include funding and space shortages. Supporters of the Simon Group suggest that students who were at risk of dropping out can eventually become high school graduates. Schools in malls may be a vanguard of the future (Molnar 2005).

SUMMARY AND CONCLUSIONS

Serious school reform efforts began at the end of the decade of the 1980s. Currently, the impact on public schools is being viewed through the implementation process of the 2001 NCLB Act. States have been mandated to retain a small percentage of their federal Title I, Part A, funds for school improvement and to provide a system of sustained support for low-performing schools. Currently, school reform and improvement varies with many creative programs and processes emerging.

Low-performing schools face sanctions for continued nonperformance. Under NCLB, Title I schools that do not meet state yearly progress levels for two consecutive years face a series of sanctions, the first being school choice, where parents are given the option to transfer their child to a higher-performing school in the district or to a charter school. Some problems have been identified in implementing transfers and only about 1 percent of the eligible students were transferring because of space in some receiving schools, the school not receiving low-performing status until midsemester, or lack of parental information. Some principals of higher-rated schools were reticent to accept transfer students from another school in their district because of turf issues. Critics of school choice suggest that transfer choice should not be a first option under NCLB because schools need an opportunity to provide student assistance before the transfer.

In the third year of not making adequate progress, schools are required to provide supplemental education in addition to school choice. Tutoring has emerged as the favored supplemental service with a range of 7 percent of the eligible students receiving tutoring in California to 49 percent in Utah, based on a review of information submitted by a sample of eight states.

Several different restructuring models have emerged, such as block scheduling, computer assisted technology, and comprehensive school restructuring into small learning communities. Small school learning communities have become popular, particularly with the assistance of large sums of money from foundations like the Bill and Melinda Gates Foundation for redesigning large comprehensive high schools into several small learning communities. Results of a program evaluation commissioned by the Gates Foundation showed mixed results and lower achievement in mathematics at Gates funded schools than traditional schools.

School takeovers by state departments of education are becoming more frequent and some takeovers have led to total school restructuring or for schools to be managed by outside private agencies or other agencies. In some large urban cities, such as Chicago and Philadelphia, schools are being managed by city mayors. Small schools in malls are becoming more popular because of school space and funding issues. These schools have been managed by private organizations.

There are many creative programs and outside agencies both private and secular competing for federal education dollars. Parental choice is the overreaching theme. There is little evidence to date that these innovations are significantly impacting student achievement. The Bush administration is a strong supporter of education change through parental choice and this focus is significantly impacting today's public schools.

How educators choose to navigate through the maze of potential reform efforts depends largely on their ability to understand the needs of the local community. The time for the one-size-fits-all model of education appears to be over and educators are faced with a host of possibilities.

CHAPTER 7 REFLECTION QUESTIONS

1. What are your school and district doing to improve collaboration efforts with the school community?

2. What steps have your school and district taken to move to an intervention model for achievement rather than one that emphasizes remediation?

3. In what ways do your school and district participate in continuous evaluation of student achievement?

4. What innovative school models has your district considered since the implementation of NCLB?

CHAPTER 7 HELPFUL WEBSITES

Accelerated Schools:
   www.acceleratedschools.org/

Agostini vs. Felton:
   www.ed.gov/legislation/ESEA/feltguid.html

Bill and Melinda Gates Foundation:
   www.gatesfoundation.org/Education/

Lafayette Square School (Indianapolis, In.):
   syf.simon.com/erc.aspx?pgID=468

Literacy Enhancement Test Sophistication:
   www.cga.ct.gov/pri/archives/1999sbfinalreport2student.htm

Mayoral Takeover of Schools:
   www.mackinac.org/pubs/mer/article.asp?ID=1680

National Network of Partnership Schools:
   www.ed.gov/pubs/ToolsforSchools/nnps.html

Numeracy Enhancement Test Sophistication:
   www.cga.ct.gov/pri/archives/1999sbfinalreport2student.htm

Professional Learning Communities (DuFour):
   info.csd.org/staffdev/rpdc/darticle.html

School Reform Commission:
   www.phila.k12.pa.us/src/

Shopping Mall Schools:
   www.learningpt.org/

Simon Property Group:
   www2.indystar.com/library/factfiles/people/s/simon/simons.html

Success for All:
   www.successforall.net/

Wilmer-Hutchins I.S.D.:
   wilmerhutchins.ednet10.net/

8

Impact of NCLB on School Finance

The art of progress is to preserve order amid change and to preserve change amid order.

—Alfred North Whitehead, British mathematician, philosopher

SCHOOL FINANCE: BACKGROUND

All fifty states with the exception of Hawaii create public school systems organized into local school districts that rely on financing from local property taxes. (Hawaii has a state school system, not separate districts.) Property taxes are based on property values that are unequally distributed across school districts and across states. Traditional school finance policy response to inequities caused by unequal property tax bases has been to restructure state financing systems to mitigate unequal effects while still maintaining the fifty-state system structures (Yudof, Kirp, Levin, and Moran 2002).

Revenue to finance K–12 education comes from state and local money with only about 6 percent to 7 percent from federal sources. Each state is responsible for K–12 education and each state school finance system is established by state law. Sometimes state Departments of Education provide regulations and complex formulas for distributing state funds. A general formula is usually applied with special formulas allocated to different populations, for example, disadvantaged or students with disabilities.

Funding allocations also vary with different types of spending such as transportation or differences among district size and costs. Some state legislatures have designed formulas to provide more money to poor districts (Yudof et al. 2002).

CURRENT STATE FUNDING REALLOCATIONS: THE EXAMPLE OF TEXAS

In 1993 the Texas Legislature passed Senate Bill 7, which established the current system of equalization known as Robin Hood. This system is found in chapter 42 of the Texas Education Code. Under this code, basic funding is divided into three major areas, called Tier 1, Tier 2, and a facilities component, Tier 3. Tier 1 is considered basic funding and amounts to $2,587 per student. In order to receive this state funding allotment, each school district must generate a local share based on $0.86 for each hundred dollars of taxable property value in the district. The basic allotment is adjusted for special education, career and technology, bilingual, and gifted and talented programs. Districts also receive an adjustment to their Tier 1 allotment to recover transportation costs and costs associated with teacher enrichment (Texas Education Code, Title II, chapter 42).

Tier 2 allotments are designed to provide a specified amount per weighted average student in state and local funds for each cent of tax effort over that required for the district's local fund assignment (Texas Education Code, Title II, chapter 42). The basic allotment is $27.14 per weighted average daily attendance, which is a weighted attendance value adjusted by the number of students participating in programs that carry additional costs (The Coalition to Invest in Texas Schools 2005). The Tier 2 tax effort is limited to $0.64 for each hundred dollars of taxable property value (Texas Education Code, Title II, chapter 42).

Facilities Allotment

Chapter 46 of the Texas Education Code governs the administration of an instructional facilities allotment for school districts making debt service payments on qualifying bond and lease purchase agreements for facility construction (Coalition to Invest 2005). The facilities component is calculated at $35 per student based on average daily attendance and is limited to $100,000 per year. The local share of these funds is raised through a $0.29 maximum rate per one hundred dollars of taxable property value (Texas Education Code, Title II, chapter 46).

Texas's Wealth Equalization Program

The most controversial aspect of Texas school funding is the wealth equalization program set forth in chapter 41 of the Texas Education Code. A school district may not have a taxable property value over $305,000 per weighted average daily attendance. Districts with taxable property values in excess of the stated cap are subject to recapture where the district is required to send excess taxes collected to the state for redistribution to low-income districts through the Foundation School Program. This requirement redistributes local tax funds out of district (Texas Education Code, chapter 41).

There are four ways Texas districts can reduce property wealth and avoid recapture. A district can voluntarily consolidate with another district whose wealth is below the $305,000 threshold. A district can detach or annex areas that will change the tax base such that the threshold is met. Most chapter 41 districts choose to purchase attendance credits from the state which is the recapture process.

Districts may choose to educate a number of nondistrict residents at a level that reduces wealth per average daily attendance, or the district may consolidate the tax base in order for two or more districts to share revenue from the newly established consolidated taxing district. Each of these options carries different fiscal requirements that make recapture the best option for most districts. This Robin Hood statute has been challenged by civil lawsuits most recently by *Neeley vs. West Orange–Cove Consolidated Independent School District*, 2004.

Projected NCLB Impact on Texas Funding

Some critics have argued that NCLB is an unfunded mandate and Congress has appropriated $30 billion less than the funding that was authorized (Lav and Brecher 2004). Other authors have identified the actual costs of implementing NCLB. Imazeki and Reschovsky (2005) studied

2002 Texas information and have estimated that it will cost $8,126 per pupil to reach the 55 percent stated passing rate standard set for 2005. Current Texas funding allocation computes to a total of $2,537 per pupil and the state expects a maximum local tax effort to contribute an additional $4,575 totaling $7,112 per pupil. This formula creates a projected shortfall of $1,014 per pupil and this deficit amounts to a $4 billion statewide shortfall to implement NCLB at the 2005 rate of 55 percent (Imazeki and Reschovsky 2005).

EDUCATION FUNDING CUTS AND DISAGREEMENTS

On December 15, 2005, the Associated Press reported that lawmakers voted to cut federal aid to education for the first time in a decade. GOP leaders promised an additional 1 percent across-the-board cut to all agency budgets. This meant about $3 billion in cuts across the budgets for the Department of Education, Labor, and Health and Human Services. Programs funded through NCLB would face a 4 percent cut, while special education and Title I would be frozen at last year's levels if these cuts are imposed (Associated Press 2005, December 15).

With the passage of the Senate Funding Bill for education, the 2006 federal budget must be reconciled with the house budget passed in May 2005. The bill contains an increase of $143 million for education or 0.25 percent above the 2005 allocation for a total of $56.7 in discretionary spending for the Department of Education. Very slight increases were approved for Title I and for IDEA under the Senate version.

Differences between this year's Department of Education federal budget when compared with President Bush's request and the House and Senate versions of amount of increase or decrease for 2006 are noted as follows:

- Title I—2005 budget: $12.74 billion.The president requested a slight increase of $0.6 billion, but both the Senate and House slashed this to $0.1 billion.
- Special Education—2005 budget: $10.59 billion. The president requested a $0.51 billion increase, but the House and Senate decreased this amount to $0.15 billion.

- Educational Technology—2005 budget: $496 million. The president did not recommend funding educational technology. The House voted to increase funding by $196 million and the Senate voted to reduce funding by $71 million.
- Striving Readers—2005 budget: $25 million. The president wanted to increase spending by $175 million, the House wanted to increase spending by $5 million, while the Senate voted to increase spending by $10 million.
- High School Intervention—2005 budget: none. This initiative was not funded this year. The president requested $1.24 billion for this item. Neither the House nor the Senate voted to fund the item in 2006.
- Teacher Incentive Fund—2005 budget: none. This initiative was not funded this year. The president requested $500 million. The House voted to spend $100 million, but the Senate voted not to fund this item in 2006.
- Vocational Education—2005 budget: $1.33 billion. The president voted to not fund vocational education in 2006. Both the House and the Senate voted to increase vocational education by $0.02 million.
- Pell Grants—2005 budget: $12.36 billion. The president requested an additional $0.87 billion for Pell grant aid in 2006. The House voted to increase Pell grants by $1.02 billion and the House voted to increase by $0.81 billion.
- Total Spending—2005 budget: $56.58 billion. The president reduced total education spending by $0.53 billion. Both the House and the Senate voted to increase education discretionary spending by $0.12 billion.

Obviously Congress did not want to scrap vocational education in favor of President Bush's high school incentives program, which included intervention plans for incoming 9th-graders who were not performing at grade level. Bush's teacher incentive plan did not appear to find favor in the Senate and the House voted only moderate support. The less than 1 percent increases for Title I and special education come at a time when NCLB is putting pressure on both programs to provide help to children to meet higher education goals.

COURT VS. STATE LEGISLATURE FUNDING ISSUES

Since 2000, tensions have increased dramatically between state courts ordering school funding reform and the state legislatures responsible for compliances with judicial orders. A number of states are headed to courtrooms based on the unfunded mandate clause. According to *Education Week*, this clause was put in three education acts in 1994. These acts included Goals 2000, the Educate America Act, and the School-to-Work Opportunities Act. Reauthorization language from the America's Schools Act was placed in the NCLB Act.

The provision stated:

> Nothing in this act shall be construed to authorize an office or employee of the federal government to mandate, direct, or control a state, local education agency, or school's curriculum, program of instruction, or allocation of state or local resources, or mandate a state or any subdivision thereof to spend any funds or incur any costs not paid for under this act. (Hendrie 2005, May 4, p. 22)

This language has become the legal weapon for a number of high-profile legal challenges to the NCLB Act.

Legal Challenges to State/Federal Funding Issues

Connecticut was the first state to use the unfunded mandate clause. Their attorney general said that the state would need to use $8 million of the state's money to fund the expansion of state achievement testing required by the NCLB Act. Similarly, the National Education Association (NEA), ten of its affiliates, and several school districts contended that NCLB is an unfunded mandate. Both Connecticut and the NEA conceded that Congress is allowed to attach conditions to federal funding.

At the heart of the argument was the price tag for compliance with federal NCLB mandates. The plaintiffs argued that upfront conditions were unclear concerning state responsibilities for local spending, as one of the conditions for state receipt of the federal money. A general counsel for the NEA stated, "If this case does nothing else, it will at least allow us to have an objective forum to decide which statements are correct—our statements that say it is under funded or the Department of Education's that say that it's adequately funded" (Hendrie 2005, May 4, p. 22).

In November 2005, the nation's largest teacher union, NEA, lost their case in their legal challenge of the NCLB Act. A federal Michigan judge ruled that Congress may require states and school districts to spend their own funds to comply with federal school improvement mandates. The judge in this case ruled that the plaintiffs had no valid federal claim.

Illinois expenditures were used by the federal attorneys as an example. Illinois is expected to spend $13 million per year to comply with NCLB test requirements, but they received $13 million in federal funds for this purpose. Wording was clarified that an officer or employee of the federal government could not impose an unfunded mandate on states and districts, but that did not limit Congress from doing so through approval of the NCLB Act. The federal judge validated the plaintiffs' right to file the case because all that was required was that the plaintiffs supply facts in support of their standing (Trotter 2005, December 7).

Archer (2005, May 25) cited findings from a Government Accountability Office (GAO) report suggesting that the key to state assessment costs was the types of tests states developed. Many states using open-ended items would not have enough money if they did not revise test item types. Open-ended items comprised 50 percent of Maine's state achievement tests. That state is considering reducing the number of open-ended items to 20 percent. The Department of Education emphasized to the states that NCLB test requirements did not require states to expand what they were using (Archer 2005, May 25).

On December 2, 2005, the U.S. Department of Education asked the U.S. District Court in Hartford, Connecticut, to dismiss Connecticut's lawsuit challenging the NCLB Act. The Department of Education argued that a state could not accept federal money for an initiative without abiding by the initiative's requirements. The Department found Connecticut's estimates of cost for implementing state testing requirements went beyond what NCLB required. Connecticut tests in grades four, six, and eight (Archer 2005, December 14).

State Finance Challenges Concerning NCLB

A number of school districts are going to court to challenge states to provide more funding to implement the NCLB mandates. In Missouri, a group of school districts is contesting the state's new funding system, saying that the new formula was underfunded. The new law tried to equalize state aid to schools by establishing a minimum funding level per student. The new formula would phase in over seven years and add an additional $800 million a year to the $2.5 billion the state now receives. The districts are contesting the new funding because of the phase-in period covering seven years before districts receive the full amount (Viadero 2005, December 7).

In Connecticut, eight school districts and fifteen students filed a class action suit against the state in November 2005, saying that the state funding formula violates the Connecticut Constitution by not providing equal education opportunity. This suit is supported by a group of mayors, school districts, and education organizations calling themselves the Connecticut Coalition for Justice in Education Funding. This coalition alleges that taxpayers are paying too much of the total funding bill for their schools. They are calling for a new state finance system that will provide adequate funds for education. The Connecticut governor stated that the Connecticut legislature should fix the problem, not court judges (Viadero 2005, December 7).

In Texas, a school finance decision was handed down by the Texas Supreme Court in October 2005, giving the state legislature a timeline to change property tax formulas for school funding. This court ruling required changes in property tax laws for Texas school finance to be constitutional. The court ruled that the $36.8 billion Texas is spending on K–12 education is enough and did not require increases for school financing.

It was noted in this court case, *Neeley vs. West Orange–Cove Consolidated Independent School District*, that achievement scores have steadily improved over time, even though both curriculum and testing requirements have been made more difficult. This court ruling is expected to generate other state challenges to state school finance systems. The significant issue with the Texas ruling is that Texas has specific constitutional requirements barring a property tax. The ruling that Texas schools are adequately funded could cause concern for other states trying to obtain more school funding (Hoff 2005, December 7).

In June 2005, the Kansas Supreme Court found that the $2.4 billion the legislature had approved for schools in 2005–2006 was not enough to provide an adequate education, which is guaranteed by the Kansas Constitution. This finding was the result of a school finance case filed in 1999 by students and districts. The court ordered the Kansas legislature to appropriate an additional $143 million for Kansas schools. In July 2005, Kansas lawmakers appropriated the $148 million after questioning the court's authority to order them to appropriate money for schools. The legislature then commissioned a study to determine how much money is needed to provide a suitable education under the Kansas Constitution (Hoff 2005, July 13).

Plaintiffs have focused on whether states provide adequate school funding since 1990. Since 2000, state budgets have been under more intense pressure from a sluggish economy and fierce public opposition to tax increases. Although state constitutions reflect what is considered an appropriate education for all children, current school funding systems reflect what states are willing to pay for education. In New York, advocates for increased school funding reentered the courtroom to try to force the legislature to enact the states' Supreme Court order to fix funding for New York City public schools. Court orders are raising constitutional questions about the limits of judicial authority and whether the court has the power to enforce its rulings (Hoff 2005, April 6).

CURRENT FUNDING ISSUES

The Colorado Referendum

In Colorado, voters passed Referendum C, which curtails for the next five years strict constitutional limits on state and local revenue, and will allow $3.7 billion to be spent on education, health care, and transportation projects. The education community expressed relief that Referendum C passed; otherwise there would have been major cuts in K–12 spending (Jacobson 2005, November 9).

State Lottery Education Funding

North Carolina became the 42nd state to endorse a lottery. The North Carolina lottery is expected to bring in more than $400 million annually. This money is slated for college scholarships, school construction, poor school districts, class-size reduction, and a preschool initiative. Fewer than half the states allocate their profits from lotteries to education. The following twelve states set lottery money aside exclusively for education: California,

Florida, Georgia, Illinois, Michigan, New Hampshire, New Jersey, New Mexico, New York, North Carolina, Ohio, and Tennessee. Opponents of state lotteries for education contend that there are no guarantees that lottery proceeds will not supplant regular education aid and may lead to perceptions among voters that school bond referendums are unnecessary. Other opponents of lotteries suggest that lotteries prey on the poorest residents, promote state gambling, and are an unreliable funding source (Manzo 2005, September 14).

Hurricane Relief Funding

Congress passed $62 billion for general federal hurricane relief, but none of that money has been allocated specifically for schools. President Bush announced the Hurricane Education Assistance Act that included $1.9 billion for school districts taking in more than ten students displaced by Hurricanes Katrina and Rita. This bill proposed to provide public schools with as much as 90 percent of their states' per-pupil expenditures for a maximum of $7,500 per student (Davis 2005, October 19).

Representative Miller from California also introduced a hurricane relief bill that would provide up to $8.2 billion for one year to public schools damaged by hurricanes. This bill would provide $8,314 per student to districts taking in displaced hurricane students (Davis 2005, October 19).

House Republican leaders proposed reopening the 2006 budget resolution passed earlier to reconsider education funding in lieu of hurricane issues. House Democrats oppose reopening the 2006 budget resolution to make cuts for hurricane aid so that at this time the school hurricane aid issue remains unresolved (Davis 2005, October 19).

TITLE I AID COULD BE MISUSED

An *Education Week* report (Hoff 2005, August 31) suggests that district budgeting practices favor schools with the fewest educational challenges and that school administrators may be unaware that Title I schools are being shortchanged. A clause in the federal Title I law allows districts to use the average of all teacher salaries districtwide in determining how the district is reimbursed from Title I funds.

The averaging process spreads program dollars for teacher salaries across the district indirectly supplementing teachers in schools not eligible for Title I funding. Grants under Title I are based on enrollments of low-income students. Teachers with the most experience and the highest salaries routinely use seniority rights to obtain jobs in schools serving higher-income students; Hoff (2005, August 31) reported that Title I teachers were paid as much as 3 percent less in the poorest schools in districts studied.

FUNDING ISSUES—SUMMARY

Since 2000, school funding issues have emerged as a major issue nationwide. Legal challenges are forcing state legislatures to reexamine state funding formulas for public school finance. State Supreme Court judges are making decisions requiring state legislatures to address funding formulas and local tax issues. Some state funding formulas based on local taxes are being challenged as unconstitutional.

At the federal level states are challenging the Education Department's authority to require states and schools to implement federal mandates without adequate funding. Funding issues resulting from displaced students because of Hurricanes Katrina and Rita are not yet resolved. Colorado voters approved a referendum overriding constitutional prohibitions on state spending for education while North Carolina has approved a state lottery to generate income for schools. Different 2006 budgets have been approved by both the House and Senate. A finance committee must now resolve major differences primarily concerning the areas of educational technology, striving readers, the teacher incentive fund, vocational education, and Pell grants. Federal funding for school budgets should be approved and available to schools for the term beginning in the fall 2006.

CONSTITUTIONALITY AND LEGAL ISSUES OF NCLB

There is little question that the NCLB Act represents unprecedented federal involvement in the affairs of the nation's public schools. NCLB supporters claim that NCLB is an effective national education reform initiative requiring intrusion into state and local education to ensure high quality, uniformity, and success, while opponents of NCLB argue that it is politically motivated and a detriment to public schools.

The purpose statement of NCLB implies sweeping federal authority ensuring that all children have equal and significant opportunity to obtain a high-quality education and placing significant proficiency standards on states for establishing and implementing accountability systems and for staffing schools with highly qualified professionals. This level of federal intrusion into an area reserved for state control raises legal questions based on the separation of powers established in the U.S. Constitution. The Tenth Amendment defines the balance of power: "The powers not delegated to the United States by the Constitution nor prohibited by it to the States, are reserved to the States respectively, or to the people" (McColl 2005, p. 605).

Spending Clause

The federal government has relied on the spending clause to assume power for establishing the NCLB Act and for most federal education policies including those that prohibit discrimination, such as Title IX–race, ethnicity, and national origin, or the Individuals with Disabilities Education Act. The spending clause (Art. 1, sec. 8, cl. 1) states: "The Congress shall have power to levy and collect Taxes, Duties, Imports and Excises, to pay the Debts and provide for the common Defense and general Welfare of the United States" (McColl 2005, p. 605).

The spending clause allows Congress to enact legislation in areas over which it otherwise has no authority if the legislation is in the form of an offer or a contract, that is, if federal funds are offered to states as an inducement to meet certain conditions. Because spending clause legislation is like a contract, provisions must be stated clearly upfront for the states to be able to decide whether or not to accept the terms. Courts have upheld use of the spending clause based upon the major premise that states voluntarily and knowingly accept the terms of the "contract." Therefore, it is crucial that individuals of the states understand the terms of the NCLB contract and have the choice to accept or reject it including federal funding with conditions.

It has been easy to conclude from the extent of the Education Department's efforts to clarify NCLB and provide guidance to the states on implementation that this law was not clear. For instance, by February 2004, the Education Department had issued more than twenty-nine guidance documents and written letters to numerous chief state school officers. In addition, the Education Department found it necessary to clarify key NCLB components such as school choice requirements, the definition of highly qualified teachers, the inclusion of students with significant cognitive disabilities, and the accountability model. From a constitutional perspective, this shows that there were many key issues that were not clear in the legislation (McColl 2005).

State Accountability Plans

The process of obtaining Education Department approval of state accountability plans has led to confusion. Two of the most controversial areas have been in testing students with severe cognitive disabilities and those who are not proficient in English. NCLB required that these students be included in AYP calculations, causing some schools to miss their AYP goals. Without clear guidance in the law itself, states elected to address assessing academic progress of these students in different ways. The Department of Education's stance on the issue of testing these students has changed over time. Some states were allowed to use different minimum numbers for calculating these subgroup populations or a higher exclusion rate. Use of a growth model is now being piloted (McColl 2005).

In addition to being confused about what was expected of them, states were uncertain about the level of funding they would receive. In funding NCLB, Congress authorized increases for Title I in a stepwise fashion, beginning with $13.5 billion in FY 2002 and increasing to $25 billion in FY 2007. In 2005, Title I was funded $12.74 billion but the authorization was for $20.5 billion, suggesting significant underfunding. The 2007 figure represented full funding based on the calculated number of children to be served.

One thing is clear about authorization levels, they do not guarantee any particular amount of funding. The disparity between funding authorized and actual funding raises a constitutional question. When NCLB was enacted, was it possible for states to knowingly accept the terms of the contract? This is a question for the courts to answer. In the past, they have tended to focus on the clarity of the contract, not the clarity of the funding. Additionally, whether the states feel pressured to accept the requirements on NCLB in order to continue receiving federal money or whether they feel this law merely offers an inducement to act needs to be investigated. NCLB mandates could be viewed as coercive (McColl 2005).

Supremacy Clause

Another legal issue emerging with the implementation of NCLB mandates is the supremacy clause (Art. VI, cl. 2) of the U.S. Constitution, stating, "This Constitution, and the Laws of the United States which shall be made in Pursuance thereof . . . shall be the supreme Law of the Land; and the judges in every State shall be bound thereby, any thing in the Constitution or Laws of any State to the Contrary notwithstanding" (McColl 2005, p. 609). In *Lawrence County vs. Lead-Deadwood School District* (1985), the court determined that the supremacy clause applied to state laws that were in conflict with federal law and also to state laws that were obstacles to the purposes and objectives of Congress.

To comply with NCLB many states have had to change laws related to their accountability systems, to high school exit exams, licensure requirements, and class-size requirements. Even state constitutions can be displaced if they are an obstacle to the accomplishment and objectives of Congress (McColl 2005).

What could happen if NCLB authority is challenged in the Supreme Court? If Congress wished to continue with the NCLB reform goals of the law, a new contract would have to be written that clearly described conditions that promote, but do not coerce states to participate. If Congress was unwilling to meet the spending clause requirements, then it would have to closely examine its intrusion into the state domain of education (McColl 2005).

Hoff (2005, March 2) discusses a report released by the National Conference of State Legislators (NCSL). The major thrust of the report suggests that Washington should give states broader authority to define student achievement goals and more latitude to devise strategies to attain them. A list of recommended changes to consider for the 2007 reauthorization of NCLB includes the following major items (Hoff 2005, April 6, p. 22):

1. Conduct Studies
   - Conduct a study to determine if NCLB is an unfunded mandate.
   - Conduct a study to calculate costs of state compliance and ensuring AYP.
2. Funding
   - Allocate an additional $18 billion per year for Title I (40 percent national per pupil funding).
3. Accountability Plans and Appeals
   - Publish decisions on states' accountability plans.
   - Set up an appeals process for states whose plans are denied.
4. Interventions for Low-performing Schools
   - Allow states to determine interventions for low-performing Title I schools instead of mandatory choice and supplemental services.
5. Testing for Special Populations
   - Let states determine the percentage of special education students tested.
   - Let states determine when to test LEP students in English.

Constitutional Issues

The NCSL's report speculates that the NCLB law is unconstitutional because the U.S. Constitution does not define a federal role for K–12 education. The report cited a 1987 Supreme Court decision that required the federal government to be unambiguous and forbade it to coerce when implementing laws in areas where it has no direct authority. The report cited numerous examples of ambiguity between the Department of Education and states requiring ongoing amendments to state plans in response to changing federal guidance. The report also noted lack of any models for states to follow in drafting accountability plans (Hoff 2005, March 2).

STATE RESISTANCE TO NCLB LAWS

Utah

The Utah state representative, Margaret Dayton, challenged NCLB on issues of states rights, last year leading a push for Utah to opt out of accepting this mandate. Only after federal officials traveled to Utah and convinced lawmakers there that the state could lose $106 million in education funds was this mandate accepted. This year Representative Dayton has devised an alternative plan asking that the state be granted a waiver to use the Utah Performance Assessment System for Students (U-PASS) as the basis for monitoring public schools, not NCLB.

A major difference between the two systems is U-PASS expects every child to make a year's worth of progress based on individual performance. NCLB requires every child to reach the same benchmarks regardless of where they start. U-PASS tests in more grades than NCLB requires but it does not emphasize performance by minority groups like NCLB. U-PASS considers other factors, such as attendance and graduation rates besides just test scores to determine a school's AYP status. The College Board's Advanced Placement Report to the Nation ranked Utah third in the nation for students who passed AYP tests (Davis 2005, February 9).

Utah officials continued resistance to NCLB mandates saying they were too invasive while federal officials say NCLB requirements were necessary for school improvement (Davis 2005, March 9). In April 2005, the Utah legislature voted to allow its state accountability system to supersede the federal NCLB mandates. This bill also directed Utah education officials to ignore any provision of federal law that was not paid for by federal funds (Keller and Sack 2005, April 27). On May 2, 2005, the governor of Utah signed the controversial bill declaring that Utah education laws would take priority over federal laws. This action could jeopardize Utah's receipt of some $76 million in federal education aid.

The Salt Lake City based Raza Political Action Coalition filed a complaint with the U.S. Department of Education's office of civil rights demanding an investigation into the achievement gap between Utah's minority students and their white peers. Raza made it clear they did not support Utah's disregard of federal accountability laws in favor of Utah's accountability system, which Raza considered one of the weakest in the country. The governor of Utah announced that he would form an achievement-gap task force to study differences in achievement scores among subgroups in Utah (Davis and Archer 2005, May 11).

Texas

When faced with a conflict between Texas laws and the federal NCLB law, Texas chose its own law, jeopardizing millions of dollars in federal education money. The major issue concerned assessment of special education students. The commissioner of education granted a number of waivers to school districts allowing them to use less stringent state rules for assessing special education students and as a result 431 districts and 1,312 schools were considered to have met AYP goals even though they did not follow NCLB rules for counting the test scores of students with disabilities.

The NCLB rule required that districts or schools were only allowed 1 percent of their enrollment to be tested against other than grade-level standards and any students above the 1 percent who did not take state tests were to be considered as not proficient for purposes of determining AYP. Texas officials noted that the Education Department did not make the 1 percent rule official until December 2003, just two months before Texas began testing. The Texas commissioner of education granted appeals to districts and schools who said their special education populations failed to reach the district's achievement targets solely because of the 1 percent rule. Without the appeals, 22 percent or 1,718 of the state's 7,813 schools would not have met AYP goals. Texas districts that did not make AYP in 2003–2004 numbered 402 (Hoff 2005, March 9).

Because of state complaints that the 1 percent rule was too low and did not address students with moderate disabilities who were unable to reach grade-level standards, the secretary of education introduced the 2 percent rule for exemptions in May 2005. NCLB requires that all students reach grade-level proficiency standards by 2013–2014 (Olson 2005, September 21).

SUMMARY AND CONCLUSIONS

The constitutionality of the NCLB law has been questioned concerning the specificity of the law with respect to contracts under the spending clause of the constitution. Clarification and revision efforts made by the Department of Education clearly show the confusion school districts and states have had in attempting to implement NCLB. Additionally, there was some evidence of federal coercion in getting Utah legislators to accept this mandate by threatening to withhold millions of dollars in federal education funds. Many states have had to amend state laws in order to comply with NCLB regulations. State legislators have speculated that the federal intrusion in public school issues is unconstitutional, although the constitutionality of this law has yet to be tested in the Supreme Court.

State legislators have identified a number of items that need to be addressed when reauthorizing NCLB in 2007. Funding levels have been questioned because of the significant $11 billion or more difference between authorized funding and actual funding for the 2006 budget for Title I leading to allegations of underfunding. Some states have actively resisted compliance with NCLB based on state rights issues for education. The Utah legislators approved a bill placing Utah's accountability system over the federal NCLB accountability system. Texas utilized their own laws when determining if school districts met their annual performance goals with respect to assessment of students in special education.

CHAPTER 8 REFLECTION QUESTIONS

1. Is it feasible for businesses to pay money for school support in lieu of city/county tax breaks?

2. Should the federal government exert pressure on education program development by awarding grants to states and local districts? Justify your response.

3. Is lottery money available to schools in your state? If not, could this become a viable source for school funding? What political actions would this take?

4. Should states shoulder more of the financial burden for local schools? If so, how would such funds be distributed equitably and ethically?

5. If businesses want students trained for the job market, what partnership responsibilities would you recommend they assume, particularly in the area of finance?

CHAPTER 8 HELPFUL WEBSITES

Chapter 41 of Texas Education Code:
www.capitol.state.tx.us/statutes/ed.toc.htm

College Board's Advanced Placement Report:
www.doe.state.de.us/news/2005/0125.shtml

Educate America Act:
www.ed.gov/legislation/GOALS2000/TheAct/index.html

Lawrence County vs. Lead-Deadwood School District:
scholar.lib.vt.edu/theses/available/etd-04212005-154751/
unrestricted/Supplanting_Dissertation_Final_Rev_1.PDF

National Conference of State Legislatures:
www.ncsl.org/

National Education Association:
www.nea.org/index.html

Pell Grants:
www.collegeboard.com/article/0,3868,6-30-0-36318,00.html

Raza Political Action Coalition:
www.freerepublic.com/focus/f-news/1412559/posts

Referendum C in Colorado:
www.americansforprosperity.org/index.php?id=354

Robin Hood (Texas School Finance Act):
files.ruraledu.org/issues/finance/news210.htm#texas

School-to-Work Opportunities Act:
www.ncrel.org/sdrs/areas/issues/envrnmnt/stw/sw3swopp.htm

Texas Foundation School Program:
www.texasimpact.com/PDFs/TASB_PSFBasics.pdf

West Orange–Cove C.I.S.D. vs. Neeley:
www.csisd.org/plugin_files/school_board/minutes/9-20-05
RegularMinutes.doc

9

High School Reform and Other Future Trends

When you declare your intention to sail in a particular direction, the winds will come strong from that direction.

—Roland Barth, educator, author

RESEARCH ON HIGH SCHOOLS

Some studies on high schools show a need for reform. Viadero (2005, February 9) reported results of two national studies on high schools for *Education Week*. Achieve, Inc., a Washington, D.C.–based group formed by governors and business leaders, conducted a survey that included opinions of both college instructors and employers suggesting that as high as 40 percent of the student respondents lacked study or job skills needed for success. Public Agenda, a nonprofit research group in New York, found that financial concerns play the major role in students' decisions to enter or remain in college. That finding was particularly true for minority students. The surveys identified student perceptions of preparation gaps particularly in mathematics. About half of the noncollege student respondents reported lack of both skills and abilities employers expected them to have. Viadero (2005) reported national statistics found that 30 percent of high school freshmen fail to earn a standard high school diploma in four years, and of those entering college, about one-fourth do not return the second year.

Reid (2005, June 22, pp. 3, 17) reports the findings of a survey conducted by the Educational Testing Service (ETS) entitled "Ready for the Real World? Americans Speak on High School Reform." The survey had 2,250 respondents including 1,037 parents, 300 high school teachers, and 300 administrators. Major findings showed that only 9 percent of the general public believed that high schools set high academic expectations for students and 30 percent believed major changes are needed in high schools. Although a growing percentage of Americans favored the NCLB law an overwhelming majority of high school teachers held unfavorable opinions of this law and opposed applying the law's strategies to raise standards and increase accountability at the high school level.

Sixty-four percent of the general public and 70 percent of the teachers supported placing greater emphasis on work-related skills such as participation in work-study programs, community service, and vocational courses to improve high schools. Parents, teachers, and administrators favored a comprehensive and rigorous academic foundation for all high school students. Results of the ETS study suggest that although more Americans appear to be in favor of the NCLB law, there is still significant opposition and many are unaware of what the legislation really means (Reid 2005, June 22).

Education Week cited a study conducted by the United Negro College Fund which interviewed sixty-two high school dropouts now in the federal Job Corps Program in West Virginia (Viadero 2005, March 23). The major reason these dropouts cited for quitting high school was mathematics. The dropouts reported being pushed along without understanding the concepts, poor teachers, not being considered smart, poor textbooks, and feelings of being bored. Viadero (2005) observes that national statistics support the fact of the struggle in math for many high school students with only 17 percent scoring at the proficient level in math on the 2000 NAEP exam. Twenty-two percent of college freshmen are identified as needing remedial math courses. Improved preparation for math teachers has been recommended if students are to be held accountable for reaching higher levels of math achievement (Viadero 2005, December 7, pp. 1, 16).

PRESIDENT BUSH'S HIGH SCHOOL PLAN

A cornerstone of President Bush's second term agenda was improving high schools. Key points of the Bush high school agenda follow (Robelen 2005, February 9, p. 24; U.S. Department of Education 2002, March).

1. More Testing
   • Require states to test students in English and math at three different grade levels instead of the one grade level now required. $250 million would be made available to states for this testing.
2. High School Intervention
   • Provide $1.2 billion to provide effective and timely intervention for below-grade-level students and hold schools accountable for teaching all students.
3. Expand "Striving Readers"
   • Increase current Striving Readers budget to $200 million. This program provides assistance to middle and high school students experiencing difficulty in reading.
4. Math and Science Teacher Development
   • Provide $269 million for the Mathematics and Science Partnership Program—a program for professional development for teachers.
5. Rigorous Curricula
   • Provide $45 million for the State Scholars Program to encourage students to take more rigorous courses. Students from low-income families would be eligible for up to $1,000 Pell grant aid for the first two years of college if they complete the State Scholars curriculum.

This high school plan calls for testing in both reading and math in grades 9, 10, and 11. Some legislators and education leaders questioned the value of still more testing and felt that the law needed better funding before Congress mandates more tests. President Bush views the expanded testing as a link to accountability like the NCLB law that is currently implemented at K–8 levels, but most high schools do not receive Title I funds so that federal funding sanctions like those applied at elementary and middle school levels would not apply to those schools. How accountability would be accomplished was not established (Robelen 2005).

Some conservative congressmen were dissatisfied with NCLB law and not willing to extend it into high schools while others were concerned about funding. The secretary of education stated that all major policy initiatives must be negotiated with the legislature (Robelen 2005, February 16).

For the first time since taking office, President Bush cut the overall budget to the U.S. Department of Education. The president sought to abolish 48 line items to make room for other priorities. Overall the cut was about 1 percent or $530 million. However, legislators did not favor shifting $1.3 billion in vocational and technical aid to support the Bush high school agenda (Robelen 2005, February 16).

HIGH SCHOOL REFORM—VOCATIONAL EDUCATION

The National Assessment of Vocational Education (NAVE) report was commissioned by Congress to examine the effectiveness of Career and Technical Education (CTE) over the past ten years. Findings suggest that CTE was very successful in improving earnings for students who enter the workforce right out of high school and for those who worked while attending college. There appeared to be a correlation with the number of CTE courses taken and increased earnings. Students who took both core academic courses and CTE courses achieved the greatest earnings.

Seven years after high school graduation, students earned about 2 percent more annually for each CTE course taken. About 25 percent of high school seniors concentrate on CTE areas, taking at least three credits in a single program area. Fifteen percent of high school seniors with a grade point average of 3.5, or higher, focused on CTE areas in 2000, although lower-achieving students were more likely to concentrate on a CTE focus (Hoachlander 2005, April 23, pp. 38, 48).

About 50 percent of the vocational students completed an academic core curriculum in 2000, an increase of about 30 percent since 1990. The number of vocational students taking a college preparatory curriculum nearly tripled since 1990. NAEP scores for CTE students increased eight points in reading and 11 points in math since 1990. Seven years after high school graduation, about 75 percent of the CTE students had participated in postsecondary training of some type and 53 percent had earned a degree or certificate. The NAVE report suggests that by adding a heavier academic load to CTE programs, students are choosing to work harder rather than give up their CTE focus (Hoachlander 2005).

Vocational curricula are not designed to produce academic learning. Little work has been done on upgrading the academic and technical content of CTE programs. Most CTE teachers have not been trained to teach academic content in CTE programs and general education teachers have not been trained to extend academic content into work-related situations. Assessment measures have not addressed CTE applications to academic learning. Public education policy will need to address the combination of CTE and academic outcomes expected and provide support for curriculum redesign, professional development, and expanded assessment if a vocational academic combination is adopted (Hoachlander 2005).

Perkins Reauthorization

On May 4, 2005, the House of Representatives overwhelmingly voted to reauthorize the Carl D. Perkins Vocational and Technical Act (Perkins III) and emphasized widespread support for vocational aid to high schools (Robelen 2005, May 11). Vocational education was one of the first federal assistance education laws passed as the Smith-Hughes Act in 1917. The Perkins III reauthorization seeks to build on reforms made in past reauthorization. The secretary of education expressed displeasure that the House bill did not stress accountability measures sufficiently. The Perkins reauthorization proposes to align academic standards with NCLB and requires local communities that received Perkins funding to establish performance indicators and improvement plans for their programs. Additionally, states would be required to evaluate programs annually against set performance standards (Robelen 2005).

Work Readiness Credential

A group of business organizations and state officials are working to establish a voluntary work readiness credential. Nine marketable skills have been identified to form the basis for this credential, which would be useful for out-of-work adults. Skills identified include speaking ability, active listening, reading with understanding, cooperation with others, resolving conflicts and negotiation skills, using math for problem solving and communications, making decisions and problem solving, critical observation skills, and taking responsibility for learning. The credential is meant to complement the high school diploma, not replace it. Adults and youths seeking to obtain such a credential would have to pass a two-and-one-half-hour online written test. Some state officials stated concern that if approved this credential could create an incentive to drop out of high school (Cavanagh 2005, February 23).

2005 GOVERNORS' SUMMIT ON EDUCATION

A state governors' summit was conducted in February 2005 to draft an action agenda for high school redesign. Three comparable education summits have been held, each providing frameworks for education policy decisions. In 1989, the nation's governors and President George H.W. Bush agreed to adopt a set of national education goals for school reform. In the 1996 summit, governors' business leaders and education supported standards-based education on a national basis.

In 1999, governors, business leaders, and education extended standards-based education to include accountability systems and teacher quality. The 2005 governors' summit encouraged states to restore value to the high school diploma by raising academic standards for students and tying graduation requirements to the expectations of employers and colleges. States were urged to set measurable goals for progress and hold high schools and postsecondary institutions accountable for outcomes. Goals and strategies for state initiatives for educational reform resulting from Governors 2005 Summit follow (Olson and Richard 2005, February 23, p. 20):

1. Restore Value to High School Diploma
   • Verify that academic standards encompass the knowledge and skills needed for successful entry-level jobs and college and university coursework.
   • Specify the core or academic content required by all students.
   • Utilize exit tests reflecting whether students are college and job ready.
2. Redesign High Schools
   • Redesign high schools to serve all students beginning with low-performing schools.

- Provide incentives for communities to expand the number of high-quality schools by supporting charter schools and expand student opportunity for dual credit with colleges and universities.
- Target time and resources for at-risk students and utilize student learning plans for at-risk students.

3. Give High School Students Excellent Teachers and Principals
   - Assist teachers to upgrade skills by changing teacher licensing requirements and preparation programs and better focus professional development money.
   - Provide state incentives for teacher recruitment and retention, particularly in math, science, and special education and hard-to-staff schools.
   - States and education leaders should collaborate to define the role of the high school principal and identify conditions for success.
   - Give principals authority to make school-level personnel and budget decisions and hold them accountable for results.

4. Set Goals, Measure Progress, and Hold High Schools and Colleges/ Universities Accountable
   - States must improve ability to collect, coordinate, and use secondary and postsecondary data.
   - States need to use multiple indicators to evaluate high schools to include graduation rates, the percentage of graduates who enroll in higher education, and the percentage who need remedial classes, as well as test scores.
   - Institutions of higher education must be required to publicly report the number of students enrolled in remedial classes, the number of dropouts after one year, as well as the number receiving a degree. States should provide incentives for those institutions that show progress.

5. Streamline and Improve Education Governance
   - States should set up a permanent commission or taskforce to frame a common education agenda for pre-15–16 and track progress.

The governors' summit urged states to make high schools both more rigorous and more personal. No one redesign model was recommended. Some large comprehensive high schools already offer rigorous college and job-ready courses. Other large high schools need to be broken up into smaller learning communities. It was also noted that fewer than ten states have data linking K–12 student records with college enrollment, while only eight states make information about student enrollment in remedial courses available. States were encouraged to include collaboration with business leaders and other stakeholders to increase a sense of urgency (Olson and Richard 2005, February 23).

A highlight of the summit was the announcement that six philanthropies to include the Bill and Melinda Gates Foundation, the Michael and Susan Dell Foundation, the Carnegie Corporation of New York, the Wallace Foundation, the Prudential Foundation, and the State Farm Foundation announced a $42 million initiative to assist states in raising high school graduation and college readiness rates. Additionally, thirteen states joined a new coalition, the American Diploma Project Network Committee, dedicated to raising standards, redesigning curricula and tying high school tests and accountability systems to knowledge and skills needed for life success after high school graduation. States involved include: Arkansas, Georgia, Indiana, Kentucky, Louisiana, Massachusetts, Michigan, New Jersey, Ohio, Oregon, Pennsylvania, Rhode Island, and Texas (Olson 2005, March 9).

Impact of Governors' Summit

The 2005 Governors' Summit has impacted states' policy on high school graduation requirements. Within six months, of the summit, several states enacted policies requiring tougher academic requirements. For example, the governor of Oklahoma signed a measure called Achieving Classroom Excellence that required all high school students to take a college-preparation curriculum beginning in 2006–2007, unless their parents sign an opt-out consent form. This legislation also required three years of math beginning with algebra I. Additionally, 9th-graders in 2008 must pass four out of six end-of-instruction tests in core academic subjects to receive a diploma. As an incentive for students, the state will pay for up to six hours of college instruction per semester (Olson 2005, June 22).

Indiana enacted similar legislation known as the Core 40 requiring students to take college-preparatory curriculum. As in Oklahoma, parents would have to request an opt-out for students to be exempt. Students with disabilities would follow their individualized education plans. Starting in

2011, high school students would have to complete the Core 40 curriculum for admission to Indiana's four year public universities. Indiana is one of the original thirteen states in the coalition formed at the summit, the American Diploma Project Network (Olson 2005, June 22).

In May, South Carolina's governor signed the Education and Economic Development Act of 2005 that will reorganize curriculum around career clusters such as health science or information technology. More states are joining the American Diploma Project Network and working on model high school curricula (Olson 2005, June 22).

EXAMPLES OF CURRENT HIGH SCHOOL REFORMS

Kansas City, Kansas—First Things First

Kansas City was the first district to utilize the First Things First model. This model has three major components: small learning communities that keep a group of students together throughout grades 9–12; a family advocate system that pairs teachers with fifteen to seventeen students for over four years; and a focus on instructional improvement. Students take core academic subjects within their learning community. This model is designed to strengthen relationships between teachers and students, broaden the role of faculty, heighten collaboration, and promote a collective responsibility for student success (Hendrie 2005, March 9).

Teachers have common planning periods daily and two hours of professional development each Wednesday when students are sent home early. Faculty decides how to allocate money and time and is responsible for assisting in filling vacancies. Teachers are designated as advocates for their group of fifteen to seventeen students meeting with them at least one hour a week and communicating with parents.

An evaluation of the program concludes that the program has had a positive impact at the high school level on graduation rates, attendance, student engagement, and test scores. This Kansas City high school was a large urban school with a student population of 1,125 with about 80 percent non-white and 75 percent qualifying for federally subsidized meals. Restructuring this high school into eight small learning communities with about 170 students each was a major change from traditional models. The project was initially awarded $2.8 million from the Kansas City, Missouri–based

Kauffman Foundation to restructure the Wyandotte High School. Recently it has received a commitment of an additional $3.8 million from the Gates Foundation for program continuation. It is considered one of the best models for restructuring high schools into smaller, more academically engaging communities (Hendrie 2005, March 9).

Chicago

With a planning grant of $2.3 million from the Gates Foundation, Chicago plans to replace sixty low-performing schools with a hundred new small schools by the end of the decade. A spokesman for the Gates Foundation said they are not insisting that the district make all high schools small, but the schools must have high academic goals for all students. In addition to the districts planning grant, the Gates Foundation announced a five year, $6 million grant to the University of Chicago's Center for Urban School Improvement to replicate a charter school it runs and to start up seven new charter high schools in the city (Hendrie 2005, May 25).

Chicago solicited proposals from outside vendors to develop core college-preparatory curriculum in the areas of English, mathematics, and science for high schools. Chicago's curriculum plan for grades 9–11 include student assessments aligned to Illinois standards and college entrance requirements. Teachers will receive related professional development and in-class coaching. Chicago is joining Boston and Philadelphia in moving toward standardization of what is taught in high schools to insure students are prepared for postsecondary education and the workforce (Reid 2005, October 5).

Texas

Since 2001, Texas high schools have offered three different high school programs. However, Texas students are encouraged to pursue one of two college-preparation programs, the recommended or the distinguished achievement. Students taking the recommended are required to take four years of English, three years of science, three years of math including Algebra II, and two years of a foreign language. The distinguished plan requires three years of a foreign language and selection from several additional options such as conducting a research project or achievement of a specified score on college-prep or college entrance exams.

Texas also has a minimum plan that requires only two years of science and no foreign language. Students receive a traditional graduation diploma regardless of the plan they follow as long as they can pass the state assessment. From 2000–2001 to 2003–2004 the percentage of students completing at least the recommended program rose from 39 percent to 64 percent. Statewide, the percentage of minority students taking at least the recommended program lags behind that of whites (Cavanagh 2005).

Texas High School Project

The Texas High School Project was initiated in 2003 by Texas Governor Rick Perry and leaders of the legislature. This initiative coordinates more than $60 million in state-managed grants for high school improvement. Several larger philanthropies to include the Bill and Melinda Gates Foundation, the Wallace Foundation, and the Michael and Susan Dell Foundation are major contributors to this project. Of the $21.5 million in grants to be announced, $8.7 million will be used to redesign five large comprehensive high schools into smaller learning communities. A large share of the money is expected to pay for contracting with a nationally recognized technical service provider who has experience in breaking up large schools into smaller ones.

Other grant money, $6.1 million, will be used to set up eight charter schools for underserved students. Several well-known management companies are competing for these funds. Of the remaining grants, $6.6 million will go to higher education systems to set up eleven schools on or near college campuses to allow students to earn two years of college credit or an associate degree while they earn a high school diploma (Trotter 2005, May 18).

OTHER STATE HIGH SCHOOL IMPROVEMENT INITIATIVES

The National Governors' Association is awarding $5.2 million to seventeen states to help improve high schools. Florida and Nevada will focus on increasing the vigor of high school courses and improve collaboration between high schools and higher education. Wisconsin will use its $500,000 to expand access to advanced placement courses between the

Madison school system and rural districts without AP classes. Kentucky and Nevada will each receive $150,000 toward building a comprehensive student data system (Hoff 2005, November 16).

RESULTS OF RESTRUCTURING HIGH SCHOOL EFFORTS

Robelen (2005) reported results of a study commissioned by the Gates Foundation to evaluate restructured high school programs. Achievement data for Gates-supported redesigned schools was limited and results of the study were reported as mixed. Overall student outcomes appeared promising for English/language arts, but mathematics progress lagged behind other schools in the same district. The quality of assignments and student work found in both new and redesigned schools was poor. There was little evidence of higher order thinking skills or deep learning. The Gates-funded schools tend to serve disadvantaged students who entered high school below grade level.

Redesigned schools showed less initial promise than start-ups. Attendance in start-ups was strong, while redesigned schools needed to address attendance. The Gates-funded schools foster close interpersonal relationships, common focus, and mutual respect and responsibility. Sustainability of some schools was threatened by staff burnout, teacher layoffs, and class-size pressure. Curriculum materials and outside guidance on teaching mathematics are needed, as well as qualified math teachers. The Gates Foundation has supported more than 850 new schools and nearly 700 existing high schools. Funding has gone to nearly 275 districts (Robelen 2005, November 16).

ACCOUNTABILITY FOR INSTITUTIONS
OF HIGHER EDUCATION

In a February 2005 speech to the America Council on Education, the Secretary of Education called upon colleges and universities to use the No Child Left Behind Act as a model for measuring the performance of institutions and reducing the achievement gap. Education advocates called this proposal for an accountability plan for higher education a bad idea. Some felt that the federal government would have a hard time defining success for colleges and universities (Honawar 2005, February 23).

Bush Commission on Future of Higher Education

In September 2005 the secretary of education appointed a Commission on the Future of Higher Education to draw up a comprehensive national strategy to ensure that the higher education system continues to meet the national need for an educated and competitive workforce for the twenty-first century. The secretary stated that she was not advocating for a bigger role for the federal government. The secretary pointed out that federal dollars made up about 33 percent of the nation's investment in higher education and that information was needed to help guide policy (Honawar 2005).

The State Higher Education Executive Officers Organization (SHEEO) formed its own commission, the National Commission on Accountability in Higher Education, to study accountability. That panel found that accountability measures currently used were cumbersome, confusing, and inefficient. The Accountability Commission recommended creating statewide data systems to inform policy and budgeting decisions and for making the transition from high school to college a focus of accountability. The secretary of education stated that her newly formed commission would consider recommendations made by the Accountability Commission (Samuels 2005, September 28).

The chairman of the Bush administration's Commission on the Future of Higher Education suggested that the commission was looking for leverage points and that he might propose making an institution's eligibility for federal student aid conditional on standardized testing. Another point under consideration was accreditation. The purpose for the commission was to devise a national strategy on higher education. The commission met in December 2005 and explored such topics as accountability and affordability. The commission must present recommendations to the secretary of education by August 1, 2006 (Field 2006, p. A39).

College Database Issues

A plan being studied by the Department of Education to create a federal database of all U.S. college students to improve graduation-rate tracking is causing privacy concerns among students and other individuals. Those who support the plan feel it could help improve policy particularly on financial aid at both federal and state levels.

A feasibility study conducted by the Institute of Education Sciences reported that data collected could help institutions of higher education compare themselves with one another, as well as help students and parents make decisions when selecting a college. Forty percent of students do not finish college at the same institution in which they started. The proposed database would maintain individual information on about sixteen million students from six thousand colleges and universities and would collect personal information to include name, social security number, date of birth, race, and gender.

Enrollment data would include courses, credits, field of study, and attendance status. Degrees awarded and dates of completion would also be included. Financial aid records and the amount of tuition and fees for each term are also requested. Such a database would have to be authorized by Congress and issues such as privacy and confidentiality would have to be addressed.

Some individuals have expressed concern about the student privacy issues and the high cost of maintaining such a database. There is a fear about the misuse of such information. Some have suggested using bar codes rather than social security numbers. This plan is still under consideration (Honawar 2005, May 11).

Higher Education Act Reauthorization

The Higher Education Act was last reauthorized in 1998. Reauthorization has twice been extended for one-year periods because lawmakers could not reach consensus on the details. Besides authorizing federal programs for student loans, grants, work-study, and institutional aid, the Higher Education Act covers programs to improve teacher preparation. A major controversy between Republicans and Democrats exists over details concerning student loans and grants. Today, about 75 percent of the federal aid goes to students in loans and the remaining 25 percent in grants. The Higher Education Act is expected to be addressed by Congress by March 31, 2006 (Honawar 2005, April 13).

Student Loans—Reconciliation Bill Passed

In December 2005, Congress passed the reconciliation bill by the narrowest of margins with the vice president casting the deciding vote. This bill must now return to the House because the Senate made minor changes. This bill has become entwined with the reauthorization of the Higher Education Act that governs student aid programs. In the reconciliation bill, congress voted to cut government-backed student loan programs by decreasing subsidies to private lenders, raising interest rates for students, and requiring borrowers to pay a 1 percent fee to agencies that guarantee loans. These cuts are the largest in student loan program history (Field 2006, January 6, p. 1).

Some new grants were approved that were tied to the areas of math, foreign language, and science. Other restrictions considered were completion of a college prep high school curriculum recognized by the secretary of education and a 3.0 grade point average. Some lobbyists have criticized the restrictions placed on new grant money, while critics are concerned that requirements could have the effect of establishing a national curriculum for all high school students. Other critics voiced concern that the program would compete for federal funds with existing student aid programs (Field 2006, p. A34).

SUMMARY AND CONCLUSIONS

Current surveys of school, community, and student stakeholders showed a need for high school reform to meet the demands of the twenty-first century. In general, the public reported awareness of the NCLB mandate and favored it, while the majority of high school teachers surveyed were unfavorable toward NCLB and opposed applying this mandate to high schools. The majority of stakeholders favored more work-related coursework for high school students. Mathematics was identified as a major weakness by students.

President Bush proposed extending the NCLB law into the high schools and holding them accountable for achievement results. Increased testing would be required in both reading and math for three grade levels instead of only one. The Bush administration is seeking leverage points for high school accountability since most high schools do not receive Title I funding. The Bush high school agenda emphasized interventions for students functioning below grade level, professional development for teachers in math and science, and a focus on a college prep curricula, and coursework in work related areas to prepare students who graduate for postsecondary education and the workplace.

A national assessment of vocational education found programs effective for increasing students' earnings in the workplace. If a combined academic and CTE program is required for high schools, curriculum redesign, professional development, and expanded assessments would need to be accomplished. The Perkins Vocational Act was reauthorized by Congress providing continued federal assistance for vocational programs.

A fourth state governors' summit designed an aggressive high school reform agenda, which began to impact state policy within six months of the summit. A number of states formed a new coalition, the American Diploma Project Network, for redesigning curricula and raising academic requirements to meet college preparation and workplace expectations. At least six states passed policy to require a college preparatory curriculum for every student, unless parents signed opt-out forms.

States are looking at assisting some large comprehensive high schools in a redesign initiative to break them into several smaller learning communities, which focus on interpersonal relationships with students, faculty collaboration, and increased parent communication with a focus on high achievement and professional development. The Bill and Melinda Gates Foundation has been instrumental in this endeavor, funding nearly 275 districts nationwide.

A program evaluation of Gates-funded start-up and redesigned small schools suggests mixed results with some improvement in English/language arts achievement, but little progress in mathematics. The Gates-funded schools primarily serve disadvantaged students who are not on grade level. The redesigned schools showed less initial promise than start-up schools, but redesign will require more time and perhaps more assistance for training and learning new ways of doing things. Outside assistance with math materials and more qualified math teachers were recommended by the Gates commissioned program evaluation.

The NCLB Act has implications for institutions of higher education (IHE's). The secretary of education has suggested that the NCLB Act be used as a model for IHE reform for accountability purposes. The Bush administration appointed a Commission on the Future of Higher Education to devise a national strategy on higher education. The Bush administration is looking for leverage points, such as institution accreditation or student loan funding, as requirements for student achievement testing for IHE accountability. A national student database is being considered as a means of tracking students from college to college, for student loan purposes, and for institution accountability.

The federal budget has become entwined in the reauthorization of the Higher Education Act because of House and Senate disagreement over details of student loan and grant funding issues. Reauthorization has not yet been accomplished. A reconciliation budget bill was passed in December 2005 by a one-vote margin. The student loan program was significantly cut to reduce federal spending; the student grant program was also decreased, but a new grant was approved with considerable NCLB-like conditions. Students would have to have a 3.0 grade point average, complete a college prep high school program recognized by the secretary of education, and major in math, science, or a foreign language.

The Bush reform agenda with its emphasis on testing is having a significant impact on public schools, although the Bush high school agenda was not funded by Congress. The impact of the 2005 governors' summit was significant on state policy for high school reform. There is little doubt that the NCLB Act will also impact both high schools and institutions of higher education in the near future as the Bush administration extends a federal role into all levels of education. More education reform efforts are clearly on the horizon.

CHAPTER 9 REFLECTION QUESTIONS

1. How will proposed NCLB changes at the high school level impact your high school?

2. What effect might these changes have on the elementary and middle schools in your area?

3. Should high school programs require both college preparation core courses and vocational/technical program courses for graduation?

4. Are high school teachers prepared to teach courses that support both vocational/technical programs and college preparation programs?

5. Should the federal government require more testing for accountability at the high school level?

6. Should high schools be penalized if their graduates are not ready for college and must take remedial courses in English and math?

7. Should the federal government exert control of college curricula and testing through withholding funding for student aid (Pell grants) or through college accreditation requirements?

CHAPTER 9 HELPFUL WEBSITES

Achieve, Inc.:
www.achieve.org/

Achieving Classroom Excellence:
www.gov.ok.gov/display_article.php?article_id=526&article_
type=1

American Council on Education:
www.acenet.edu//AM/Template.cfm?Section=Home

Bill and Melinda Gates Foundation:
www.gatesfoundation.org/Education/

Career and Technical Education:
www.acteonline.org/

Carl D. Perkins Vocational and Technical Education Act:
www.ed.gov/offices/OVAE/CTE/perkins.html

Carnegie Corporation of New York:
www.carnegie.org/

Commission on the Future of Higher Education:
www.ed.gov/news/pressreleases/2005/09/09192005.html

Core 40 (Indiana):
www.doe.state.in.us/core40/welcome.html

Education and Economic Development Act of 2005 (South Carolina):
www.oconee.k12.sc.us/business/news10_18_05.htm

Educational Testing Service: Ready for the Real World:
www.daggett.com/VYCUV2.htm

First Things First:
www.irre.org/ftf/

Governors' 2005 Summit:
www.nga.org/portal/site/nga

Higher Education Act Reauthorized 1998:
usinfo.state.gov/usa/infousa/educ/files/hiedact.pdf

CHAPTER 9 HELPFUL WEBSITES (*continued*)

Job Corps Program:
  jobcorps.dol.gov/

Kauffman Foundation:
  www.kauffman.org/

Michael and Susan Dell Foundation:
  www.msdf.org/

National Assessment of Vocational Education:
  www.ed.gov/rschstat/eval/sectech/nave/naveexesum.pdf

National Commission on Accountability in Higher Education:
  www.sheeo.org/account/comm-home.htm

National Governors Association:
  www.nga.org/portal/site/nga

Prudential Foundation:
  www.vpr.net/support_vpr/matching_grants/prudential.pdf

Public Agenda:
  www.publicagenda.org/

State Farm Foundation:
  www.statefarm.com/foundati/foundati.htm

State Higher Education Executive Officers Association:
  www.infolit.org/members/sheeo.htm

Texas High School Project:
  www.cftexas.org/thsp.html

United Negro College Fund:
  www.uncf.org/

Wallace Foundation:
  www.wallacefoundation.org/WF/

Conclusion

It is not so much where we stand, as in what direction we are moving.
To reach the port of heaven, we must sail sometimes with the wind and
sometimes against it—but we must sail, and not drift, nor lie at anchor.

—Oliver Wendell Holmes, jurist, writer

Student achievement is a major national issue for public school reform.
The NCLB Act has utilized state accountability systems to force public
schools to focus on achievement outcomes for all students. At no time in
the history of public education has a federal law achieved such widespread notoriety from preschool programs to college and university programs through use of change as a framework for transition into an unpre-
dictable future. As a result, a number of trends have emerged that have
implications for schools, school systems, colleges, universities, and other
institutions to include communities even worldwide.

The achievement gap between white students and students of color is
a major focus of the NCLB Act. For some states the population is changing through immigration and the higher birth rates of some ethnic
groups. In 2100, the number of non-Hispanic whites is expected to drop
to 40.3 percent instead of 71.4 percent reported in 2000 (Marx 2006)
suggesting that majorities will become minorities, creating ongoing
challenges for education. Traditional education was based on the twen-
tieth century's industrial needs, but educators now must get students
ready for a different economy with global implications that require

151

awareness of and sensibility to ethical dimensions, technological savvy, and understanding of different cultural backgrounds.

High schools are being restructured to become smaller learning communities with an emphasis upon leading-edge career, technical, and vocational education as well as college preparation. Educators are now pressed to offer a curriculum that addresses real world problems, questions that matter, ethics, and social justice.

Standards and higher-stakes testing have precipitated a need to personalize education programs to balance student interests, abilities, and aspirations with the needs of society and to ensure that standards do not limit the curriculum or even push students out of school. Schools and universities need to become centers for continuing education, training, and re-training teachers for today's classrooms as well as those of the future.

Research must become important and helping students turn data and information into usable knowledge must be valued. Applying the knowledge we have from cognitive research as well as other research areas from across disciplines will be necessary.

Educators need professional development programs that go beyond workshops, so that continuous improvement can replace quick fixes and defense of the status quo. Educators and communities need real understanding of the role poverty has played in our history and the challenges it poses for the future.

In line with the promises and problems of NCLB, most recently a bipartisan commission is being created to examine this law's problems and promises. Funding has become a major issue because the Bush administration has proposed a $3.2 billion cut in the 2007 education budget.

The NCLB Act may be the catalyst needed to pressure educators to become future thinkers and planners so that students may be prepared for jobs and careers that may not currently even exist. Whether it is viewed as a positive or a negative, one thing is for certain, the NCLB Act, by putting the spotlight on academic achievement, is certainly the catalyst for educators to closely examine the practice of educating students. If we consider the safe harbor to be an educated citizenry, then navigating through NCLB or any reform is critical to this goal. Educators must keep sailing forward.

References

ACORN. 2004. "Accountability Left Behind: While Children and Schools Face High Stakes Testing, Tutoring Companies Get a Free Ride." Retrieved November 21, 2005, www.acorn.org/filesadmin/ACORN_Reports/Accountability _Left_Behind.pdf.

Alan, R. 2005, February 16. "Groups Tackle Teacher Quality in Needy Schools." *Education Week* 24, no. 23: 5.

Alexander, L. 2002. "A Horse Trade for K–12 Education." *Phi Delta Kappan* 83, no. 9: 698–99.

Alliance for School Choice. 2005, September 22. *Alliance for School Choice Welcomes Bipartisan Education Relief Bill.* Retrieved November 18, 2005, www.allianceforschoolchoice.org.

Archer, J. 2005. December 14. "Education Department Seeks Dismissal of NCLB Lawsuit." *Education Week* 25, no. 15: 4.

———. 2005, July 27. "Educators See Classroom Visits as Powerful Learning Too." *Education Week* 24, no. 43: 22.

———. 2005, May 25. "State Cost Estimates Inflate Price of Tests, Federal Officials Say." *Education Week* 24, no. 38: 1, 21.

Associated Press. 2005, December 15. "House Passes Cuts to Education, Social Programs." *The Beaumont Enterprise*, 3A.

Belfield, C., and H. Levin. 2002, December. *What Does the Supreme Court Ruling on Vouchers Mean for School Superintendents?* Arlington, Va.: American Association of School Administrators. Retrieved November 21, 2005, www.ncspc.org.

Bodrova, E., and D. J. Leong. 2005. "Uniquely Preschool." *Educational Leadership* 630, no. 1: 44–47.

Bracy, G. W., and A. Stellar. 2003. "Long-term Studies of Preschool: Lasting Benefits Far Outweigh Costs." *Phi Delta Kappan* 84, no. 10: 780–83, 797.

Bush, G. W. 2005, March. *No Child Left Behind: Expanding the Promise—Guide to President Bush's FY2006 Education Agenda.* Washington, D.C.: U. S. Department of Education, Office of the Secretary. P. 1.

Cavanagh, S. 2005, August 10. "Group Seeks Federal Probe of Reading First." *Education Week* 24, no. 44: 2, 20.

———. 2005, April 20. "Several States Making College-prep Courses the Default Curriculum." *Education Week* 24, no. 32: 1, 13.

———. 2005, February 23. "Concept of Work Readiness Credential Gains Supporters." *Education Week* 24, no. 24: 19.

Cavazos, L. 2002. "Emphasizes Performance Goals and High-quality Education for All Students." *Phi Delta Kappan* 83, no. 9: 690–97.

The Coalition to Invest in Texas Schools. 2005. *Texas Schools—A Closer Look.* Retrieved June 30, 2005, www.investintexasschools.org/whats_new/files/2004/april/closer_look.pdf.

Darling-Hammond. 2001, October 15. "The Research and Rhetoric on Teacher Certification: A Response to 'Teacher Certification Reconsidered.'" National Commission on Teaching and America's Future. Available at www.nctaf.org

Davis, M. R. 2005, December 2. "Senate OK's Modest K–12 Spending Boost." *Education Week* 25, no. 10: 24, 26.

———. 2005, November 4. "Senate Okays Hurricane-aid Plan for Schools: Private School Students Included in $1.66 Billion Bill." *Education Week.* Retrieved November 6, 2005, www.eduweek.org.

———. 2005, October 19. "Cuts Weighed to Pay for Hurricane Relief." *Education Week* 25, no. 8: 22, 25.

———. 2005, October 19. "For Education Department, Hurricane Issues Are a Top Priority." *Education Week* 25, no. 8: 23.

———. 2005, June 15. "Head Start Has 'Modest' Impact, Study Says." *Education Week* 24, no. 40: 21, 23.

———. 2005, May 25. "GAO Questions Head Start Test System." *Education Week* 24, no. 38: 26.

———. 2005, May 25. "House Committee Okays Head Start Reauthorization." *Education Week* 24, no. 38: 24, 26.

———. 2005, May 11. "Complaint Targets Utah NCLB Law." *Education Week* 24, no. 36: 22.

———. 2005, March 23. "Oversight of Local Head Start Programs Flawed, GAO Says." *Education Week* 24, no. 28: 23.

———. 2005, March 9. "Utah Legislators Delay Action on NCLB Bill." *Education Week* 24, no. 26: 18.

——. 2005, February 9. "Utah Is Unlikely Fly in Bush's School Ointment." *Education Week* 24, no. 22: 1, 21.

Davis, M. R., and J. Archer. 2005, May 11. "Complaint Targets Utah NCLB Law." *Education Week* 24, no. 36: 22.

Davison, M. L., S. S. Young, E. C. Davenport Jr., D. Butterbaugh, and L. J. Davison. 2004. "When Do Children Fall Behind? What Can Be Done?" *Phi Delta Kappan* 85, no. 10: 752–61.

Digest of Education Statistics. 2004. nces.edu.gov/progrtams/digest/&04/index.asp.

DuFour, R. 2004. "What Is a Professional Learning Community?" *Educational Leadership* 61, no. 8: 6–11.

Elam, S. M. 1999. "Florida's Voucher Program: Legislating What Can't Be Done by Referendum." *Phi Delta Kappan* 81, no. 1: 81–88.

Elmore, R. F., and S. H. Fahrman. 2001. "Holding Schools Accountable: Is It Working?" *Phi Delta Kappan* 83, no. 1: 67–72.

Epstein, J. L., and K. C. Salinas. 2004. "Partnering with Families and Communities." *Educational Leadership* 61, no. 8: 12–18.

Evans, P. M. 2003. "A Principal's Dilemma: Theory and Reality of School Redesign." *Phi Delta Kappan* 84, no. 6: 425–37.

Fagan, A. 2005, October 28. "Plan to Repair Schools for Katrina Aid Rejected." *The Washington Times*. Retrieved November 6, 2005, www.washingtontimes.com.

Ferguson, R. F., and J. Mehta. 2004. "An Unfinished Journey: The Legacy of Brown and the Narrowing of the Achievement Gap." *Phi Delta Kappan* 85, no. 9: 656–69.

Field, K. 2006, January 6. "Federal Panel Appears Likely to Call for Testing of College Students." *The Chronicle of Higher Education* L11, no. 18: 1, A34, A36.

Finn, C. E., and M. Kanstoroom. 2002. "Do Charter Schools Do It Differently?" *Phi Delta Kappan* 84, no. 1: 59–62.

Florida Department of Education. 2004. *2004 Yearly Progress.* Retrieved June 20, 2005, web.fldoe.org/nclb/0304/default.cfm?action=report&level=state.

Fowler, F. 2004. *Policy Studies for Educational Leaders: An Introduction.* Upper Saddle River, NJ: Pearson Prentice Hall.

French, D. 1998. "The State's Role in Shaping a Progressive Vision of Public Education." *Phi Delta Kappan* 80, no. 3: 185–90.

Friedman, M. 1962. *Capitalism and Freedom.* Chicago: University of Chicago Press.

Garn, G. 1998. "The Thinking Behind Arizona's Charter Movement." *Educational Leadership* 56, no. 2: 48–50.

Gewertz, C. 2005, November 16. "Education Department Grants N.Y.C., Boston Waivers on NCLB Tutoring." *Education Week* 25, no. 12: 13.

———. 2005, October 19. "New Orleans Adopts Plan for Charters." *Education Week* 25, no. 8: 1, 18.

———. 2005, September 7. "Education Department Allows Chicago to Provide NCLB Tutoring." *Education Week* 25, no. 2: 3, 18.

———. 2005, June 22. "Guide Seeks New Clarity on Tutoring—Ed. Dept. Spells Out Roles for States, School Districts." *Education Week* 24, no. 41: 1, 35.

———. 2005, April 20. "Critics Question Use of Offshore Firms for Online Tutoring." *Education Week* 24, no. 32: 14.

———. 2005, April 6. "Urban Districts Report Study Academic Gains." *Education Week* 24, no. 30: 5.

Gordon, E. E. 2003. "Looking Beyond the Stereotypes: Ensuring the True Potential of Tutoring." *Phi Delta Kappan* 84, no. 6: 456–59.

Harris, S., and S. Lowery, eds. 2002. *A School for Every Child: School Choice in America Today.* Lanham, MD: Scarecrow Press.

Hart, B., and T. R. Risley. 1995. *Meaningful Differences in the Everyday Experience of Young American Children.* Baltimore: Paul H. Brookes.

Hatch, J. A. 2002. Accountability Showdown: Resisting the Standards Movement in Early Childhood Education. *Phi Delta Kappan* 83, no. 6: 457–62.

Hendrie, C. 2005, May 25. "Chicago H. S. Plan to Rethink Role for District." *Education Week,* 24, no. 38: 6.

———. 2005, May 4. "NCLB Cases Face Hurdles in the Courts." *Education Week* 24, no. 34: 1, 22.

———. 2005, April 20. "NCLB Transfer Policy Seen as Flawed." *Education Week* 24, no. 32: 1, 14–15, 22.

———. 2005, March 9. "First Things First Shows Promising Results." *Education Week* 24, no. 26: 1, 13.

———. 2005, February 16. "Texas Urged to Beef Up Oversight of Poor Charter Schools." *Education Week* 24, no. 23: 13.

Hoachlander, G. 2005, April 23. "Does Vocational Education Have a Role to Play in High School Reform?" *Education Week* 24, no. 33: 48, 38.

Hoff, D. J. 2005, December 7. "Texas School Finance Ruling Draws National Attention." *Education Week* 25, no. 14: 25, 27.

———. 2005, November 16. "States Get Private Funds to Pursue Initiatives to Improve High Schools." *Education Week* 25, no. 12: 22.

———. 2005, August 31. "Study: District Budget Practices Can Siphon Title I Aid from Poor." *Education Week* 25, no. 1: 30.

———. 2005, July 13. "Kentucky Lawmakers Agree on Spending Plan." *Education Week* 4, no. 42: 23, 26.

———. 2005, May 18. "Texas Chief Ousts Troubled District's Elected Board." *Education Week* 24, no. 37: 3, 11.

———. 2005, April 13. "States to Get New Options on NCLB Law." *Education Week* 24, no. 31: 1, 38.

———. 2005, April 6. "States Resist Meeting K–12 Spending Levels Ordered by the Courts." *Education Week* 24, no. 30: 1, 22.

———. 2005, March 9. "Texas Stands Behind Own Testing Rule." *Education Week* 24, no. 26: 1, 23.

———. 2005, March 2. "NCLB Law Needs Work, Legislators Assert." *Education Week* 24, no. 25: 1, 20.

———. 2005, May 4. "Education Department Fines Texas for NCLB Violation." *Education Week* 24, no. 34: 27–28.

Holland, R. 2005, November 1. *NEA Opposes Proposed Katrina Relief Plan for School Children.* The Hartland Institute. Retrieved October 26, 2005, www.heartland.org.

Honawar, V. 2005, November 9. "India Becoming Online Hub for Tutoring U.S. Students." *Education Week* 25, no. 11: 8.

———. 2005, May 11. "U.S. College-database Idea Sparks Privacy Worries." *Education Week* 24, no. 36: 26, 30.

———. 2005, April 13. "Hope Springs Eternal for New Higher Education Act." *Education Week* 24, no. 31: 39, 41.

———. 2005, February 23. "Spellings Backs Accountability in Higher Education." *Education Week* 24, no. 24: 29, 32.

Houston, P. D. 2005. "NCLB: Dreams and Nightmares." *Phi Delta Kappan* 86, no. 6: 469–70.

Illinois State Board of Education. n.d. Available at www.isbe.state.il.us.

Imazeki, J., and A. Reschovsky. 2005. *Does No Child Left Behind Place a Fiscal Burden on the States? Evidence from Texas.* La Follete School of Public Affairs working papers series, No. 2005–06. Retrieved July 5, 2005, www.lafollette .edu/publications/workingpapers.

Jacobson, L. 2005, November 9. "Colorado Voters Suspend Revenue Limits." *Education Week* 25, no. 11: 23–24.

———. 2005, October 26. "Charters with Native Hawaiian Focus Get Aid Infusion." *Education Week* 25, no. 9: 26.

———. 2005, October 15. "Pre-kindergarten Profit in School Finance Cases Grows." *Education Week* 25, no. 6: 18, 22.

———. 2005, September 21. "New York City Adds Pre-kindergarten Slots as State Plan Stalls." *Education Week* 25, no. 4: 26, 28.

———. 2005, August 31. "Florida Pre-kindergarten Push Raises Questions over Teacher Training." *Education Week* 25, no. 1: 23, 27.

———. 2005, July 22. "Study Urges Work on Kindergarten Policy." *Education Week* 24, no. 43: 26, 30.

——. 2005, May 18. "Preschoolers Expelled from School at Rates Exceeding That of K–12." *Education Week* 24, no. 37: 1, 12.

——. 2005, April 20. "Flurry of Activity Taking Place on Pre-kindergarten Front." *Education Week* 24, no. 32: 8.

——. 2005, February 23. "New Report Concludes School Readiness Data Needs More Attention." *Education Week* 24, no. 24: 13.

Jennings, J. F. 2000. "Title I: Its Legislative History and Its Promise." *Phi Delta Kappan* 81, no. 7: 516–22.

Kaplan, L. S., and W. A. Owing. 2003. "No Child Left Behind: The Politics of Teacher Quality." *Phi Delta Kappan* 84, no. 9: 679–86.

Kelleher, J. 2003. "A Model for Assessment-driven Professional Development." *Phi Delta Kappan* 84, no. 10: 751–56.

Keller, B. 2005, May 25. "Va. to Provide Bonuses for Middle-grades Math Teachers." *Education Week* 24, no. 38: 5.

Keller, B., and J. L. Sack. 2005, April 27. "Union States Wage Frontal Attack on NCLB." *Education Week* 24, no. 33: 1, 18.

Kirst, M., and K. Bulkley. 2004. "New, Improved Mayors Take Over City Schools." *Phi Delta Kappan* 81, no. 7: 538–46.

Lav, I. J., and A. Brecher. 2004, August 18. *Passing Down the Deficit: Federal Policies Contribute to the Severity of the State Fiscal Crisis.* Washington, DC: Center on Budget and Policy Priorities.

Manzo, K. K. 2005, November 9. "Inspector General to Conduct Broad Audits of Reading First." *Education Week* 25, no. 11: 10.

——. 2005, October 12. "GAO Probe Federal Plan for Reading." *Education Week* 25, no. 7: 1, 22.

——. 2005, September 14. "N.C. Backs Lottery to Fund School Projects." *Education Week* 25, no. 3: 28, 30.

——. 2005, July 27. "States and Districts Send Literacy Coaches to the Rescue." *Education Week* 24, no. 43: 20.

——. 2005, June 22. "Complaint Filed against Reading First Initiative." *Education Week* 24, no. 41: 3.

——. 2005, June 8. "States Report Reading First Yielding Gains." *Education Week* 24, no. 39: 1, 17.

——. 2005, May 25. "Court Showdown Over Florida Vouchers Nears." *Education Week* 24, no. 38: 1, 22–23.

McColl, A. 2005. "Tough Call: Is No Child Left Behind Constitutional?" *Phi Delta Kappan* 86, no. 8: 604–10.

Marx, G. 2006. "An Overview of Sixteen Trends, Their Profound Impact on Our Future." Austin, TX: Texas Association of School Administrators.

Mendez, A. J. 1999. "Voters versus Vouchers: An Analysis of Referendum Data." *Phi Delta Kappan* 81, no. 1: 76–80.

Metcalf, K. K., and P. A. Tait. 1999. "Free Market Policies and Public Education: What Is the Cost of Choice?" *Phi Delta Kappan* 81, no. 1: 65–68.

Miller, M. 1999, July. "A Bold Experiment to Fix City Schools." *Atlantic Monthly* 284.

Miner, B. 1998. "Why I Don't Vouch for Vouchers." *Educational Leadership* 56, no. 2: 40–42.

Molnar, A. 2005. "Ivy-covered Malls and Creeping Commercialism." *Educational Leadership* 62, no. 5: 74–79.

National Center for Education Statistics. 2005. Available at nces.ed.gov/nations reportcard/nrc/reading_math_2005/2006.asp.

National Governors Association Center for Best Practices. 2005. "NCLB: Supplemental Services Promising Practices." Available at www.nga.org/center/divisions/1,1188,C_ISSUE_BRIEF^D_5267.00.html.

Odden, A. 2000. "The Costs of Sustaining Educational Change through Comprehensive School Reform." *Phi Delta Kappan* 81, no. 6: 433–38.

Olson, L. 2005, October 26. "NAEP Gains Are Elusive in Key Areas: Friends and Foes Question NCLB Law's Effectiveness." *Education Week* 25, no. 9: 1, 22.

———. 2005, October 19. "Small States Find Benefits in Jointly Developed Tests." *Education Week* 26, no. 8: 1, 14.

———. 2005, September 21. "AYP Rules Miss Many in Special Education." *Education Week* 25, no. 4: 1, 24.

———. 2005, September 21. "New Rules on Special Ed. Scores Help Schools Meet NCLB Targets." *Education Week* 25, no. 4: 25.

———. 2005, September 7. "Defying Predictions, State Trends Prove Mixed on Schools Making NCLB Targets." *Education Week* 25, no. 2: 1, 26–27.

———. 2005, September 7. "NCLB Continues to Challenge Schools in 2005." *Education Week* 25, no. 2: 27.

———. 2005, September 7. "NCLB Waiver Lets Virginia Offer Tutoring before Choice." *Education Week* 25, no. 2: 26.

———. 2005, July 13. "Education Department Convenes Working Group on 'Growth' Models." *Education Week* 24, no. 42: 20–21.

———. 2005, July 13. "Requests Win More Leeway under NCLB." *Education Week* 24, no. 42: 1, 20.

———. 2005, June 22. "States Raise the Bar for High School Diploma." *Education Week* 24, no. 41: 1, 28.

———. 2005, April 6. "NCLB Study: State Support for Schools' Improvement Varies." *Education Week* 24, no. 30: 9.

160

———. 2005, March 23. "States Hoping to 'Grow' into AYP Success." *Education Week* 24, no. 28: 15–20.

———. 2005, March 16. "Most States Give Most Teachers 'Highly Qualified' Status." *Education Week* 24, no. 27: 20.

———. 2005, March 9. "Summit Fuels Push to Improve High Schools." *Education Week* 24, no. 26: 1, 13.

———. 2005, May 25. "Florida Gains Flexibility on NCLB Provisions: Fewer Schools Likely to Miss Annual Progress Goals under Changes." *Education Week* 24, no. 38: 18–20.

Olson, L., and A. Richard. 2005, February 23. "High Schools in Limelight for Summit." *Education Week* 24, no. 24: 1, 20, 22.

Paige, R. 2002. "The Secretary's Annual Report on Teacher Quality: Meeting the Qualified Teacher Challenge."Washington, DC: U.S. Department of Education, p. 8. Available at www.ed.gov/offices/OPE/News/teacherprep/indes.html.

Palmer, L. B., and R. Gau. 2005. "Charter School Authorizing: Policy Implications from a National Study." *Phi Delta Kappan* 86, no. 5: 352–57.

Pressley, M. 2005, December 14. "The Rocky Year of Reading First." *Education Week* 25, no. 15: 24–25.

Quality Counts. 2001, January 11. "A Better Balance: Standards, Tests, and the Tools to Succeed." *Education Week* 20, no. 17: 81–84.

———. 1999, January 11. "Rewarding Results, Punishing Failure." *Education Week* 18, no. 17: 123.

Ramirez, A. 1998. "Vouchers and Voodoo Economics." *Educational Leadership* 56, no. 2: 36–39.

Reid, K. S. 2005, October 5. "Chicago Latest District to Call for Core H.S. Curricula." *Education Week* 25, no. 6: 3, 15.

———. 2005, June 22. "ETS Poll Finds Support for Changes to High Schools." *Education Week* 24, no. 41: 3, 17.

Richard, A. 2005, December 7. "Supplemental Help Can Be Hard to Find for Rural Students." *Education Week* 25, no. 14: 1, 22.

———. 2005, February 16. "Groups Tackle Teacher Quality in Needy Schools." *Education Week* 24, no. 23: 5.

Richard, A., and C. A. Samuels. 2005, February 23. "Legislatures Hit with Surge in School Choice Plans." *Education Week* 24, no. 24: 8.

Riley, R. W. 2002. "Education Reform on America's Education Agenda." *Phi Delta Kappan* 83, no. 9: 700.

Robelen, E. W. 2005, December 7. "Ohio Supreme Court to Rule on Charter Law." *Education Week* 25, no. 14: 25, 27.

———. 2005, November 16. "Gates High Schools Get Mixed Review in Study." *Education Week* 25, no. 12: 1, 20.

———. 2005, May 11. "House Approves Perkins Reauthorization." *Education Week* 24, no. 36: 26, 30.

———. 2005, February 16. "Cuts Proposed in Bush Budget Hit Education." *Education Week* 24, no. 23: 1, 35.

———. 2005, February 16. "Bush's High School Plan Off to Rocky Start." *Education Week* 24, no. 23: 32, 34.

———. 2005, February 9. "Bush's High School Agenda Faces Obstacles." *Education Week* 24, no. 22: 21, 22.

Sack, J. L. 2005. "Teachers: Point System Available to Earn 'Qualified' Status." *Education Week* 25, no. 10: 16.

Samuels, C. A. 2005, September 28. "Spellings Drafts Panel to Study Higher Education." *Education Week* 25, no. 5: 24, 26.

———. 2005, August 16. "Subject Qualification Verifying for Teachers in Special Education." *Education Week* 24, no. 23: 1, 22–23.

———. 2005, May 18. "Special Education Test Flexibility Detailed." *Education Week* 24, no. 37: 22.

———. 2005, February 16. "Subject Qualification Vexing for Teachers in Special Education." *Education Week* 24, no. 23: 1, 22–23.

Samuels, C. A., and K. S. Reid. 2005, July 13. "Ohio Enacts Voucher Expansion, New Limits, for Charters." *Education Week* 24, no. 42: 22, 25.

Scheurich, J. J., L. Skrla, and J. F. Johnson. 2000. "Thinking Carefully about Equity and Accountability." *Phi Delta Kappan* 83, no. 9: 700–707.

Slack, J. L. 2005, March 23. "Progress Report on 'No Child' Law Shows Hits and Misses." *Education Week* 24, no. 28: 9.

Stewart, R. A., and J. L. Brendefur. 2005. "Analyzing Classroom Practice Fusing Lesson Study and Authentic Achievement: A Model for Teacher Collaboration." *Phi Delta Kappan* 86, no. 9: 681–87.

Texas Education Agency. 2005. *2005 Accountability Manual.* Available at www.tea.state.tx.us.

Texas Education Code, Title II, chapter 42.

Trotter, A. 2005, December 7. "Suit Challenging NCLB Cost Is Dismissed." *Education Week* 25, no. 14: 28.

———. 2005, May 18. "Public-private Effort Helps Texas High Schools." *Education Week* 25, no. 37: 5.

U. S. Department of Education. 2004. "Higher Education Act Title II Reporting System." In *Education Week* (2005, October 5): 13 ("High Quality Disparities").

————. 2002, September. *No Child Left Behind: A Desktop Reference*. Washington, D.C.: Office of Elementary and Secondary Education. Available at www.ed.gov/offices/OESE/reference; www.ed.gov/public/edpubs/html.

————. 2002, March. *No Child Left Behind: Expanding the Promise—A Guide to President Bush's FY 2006 Education Agenda*. Available at www.edpubs.org.

Utah State Board of Education. n.d. Available at: www.usoe.k12.tx.us/eval.

Viadero, D. 2005, December 7. "Finance Suits Being Pursued in Conn., Mo." *Education Week* 25, 14: 27.

————. 2005, October 5. "Certified Urban Educators Seem Less Likely to Be Put in 9th-grade Classrooms." *Education Week* 24, no. 32: 9.

————. 2005, July 27. "Scholars Identify Traits of Training That Lifts Student Performance." *Education Week* 24, no. 43: 18–19.

————. 2005, April 20. "Certified Urban Educators Seen Less Likely To Be Put in 9th-grade Classrooms." *Education Week* 24, no. 32: 9.

————. 2005, March 23. "Math Emerges as Big Hurdle for Teenagers." *Education Week* 24, no. 28: 1, 16.

————. 2005, February 9. "Studies Show High Schools' Shortcomings." *Education Week* 24, no. 22: 1, 12.

Vogler, K. E., and R. J. Kennedy Jr. 2003. "A View from the Bottom: What Happens When Your School System Ranks Last?" *Phi Delta Kappan* 84, no. 6: 446–48.

Wasik, B. A. 1997. "Volunteer Tutoring Programs: Do We Know What Works?" *Phi Delta Kappan* 79, no. 4: 282–87.

Wells, A. S., and Research Associates. 1998. "Charter School Reform in California: Does It Meet Expectations?" *Phi Delta Kappan* 80, no. 4: 305–12.

Whittle, C. 2005. "The Promise of Public/Private Partnerships." *Educational Leadership* 62, no. 5: 34–36.

Wiener, R., and D. Hall. 2004. "Accountability Under No Child Left Behind." *The Clearing House* 78, no. 1: 17–21.

Witte, J. F. 1999. "The Milwaukee Voucher Experiment: The Good, the Bad, and the Ugly." *Phi Delta Kappan* 81, no. 1: 59–64.

Wright, P. W. D., P. D. Wright, and S. W. Heath. 2004. *Wrights Law: No Child Left Behind*. Hartfield, VA.: Harbor House Law Press, Inc.

Yudof, M. G., D. L. Kirp, B. Levin, and R. E. Moran. 2002. *Educational Policy and the Law*. 4th ed. Bellmont, CA: Wadsworth Group/Thomson Learning.

Zehr, M. A. 2005, March 23. "Federal Data Show Gains on Language." *Education Week* 24, no. 28: 1, 25.

Zollers, N. J., and A. K. Ramanthan. 1998. "For-profit Charter Schools and Students with Disabilities." *Phi Delta Kappan* 80, no. 4: 297–304.

About the Authors

E. Jane Irons is professor of educational leadership at Lamar University in Texas with an Ed.D. from Northeastern University in Boston. She has more than thirty years of experience in public education, in which she has worked as a mathematics teacher, elementary school principal, educational diagnostician, school psychologist program director, and special education program director. She works closely with the No Child Left Behind District Office in Texas. Dr. Irons has published widely in journal articles on the topics of special education, discipline, teacher leadership, and No Child Left Behind.

Sandra Harris is director of Lamar University's Center for Research and Doctoral Studies in Educational Leadership with a Ph.D. from the University of Texas at Austin. She has worked for more than thirty years in public and private education, as a K–12 teacher, reading specialist, principal, and superintendent. Dr. Harris has published widely in books and journal articles on the topics of bullying, school leadership, and relationship-building.